CEDAR MILL COMM. LIBRARY

D0442845

QUOTABLE
WOMEN
OF THE
TWENTIETH
CENTURY

QUOTABLE WOMEN OF THE TWENTIETH CENTURY

❧

Edited by Tracy Quinn

INTRODUCTION BY CATHLEEN BLACK

WILLIAM MORROW AND COMPANY, INC.

NEW YORK

Copyright © 1999 Bill Adler Books, Inc.

All rights reserved. No part of this book may be reproduced or utilized in any form or by any means, electronic or mechanical, including photocopying, recording, or by any information storage or retrieval system, without permission in writing from the Publisher. Inquiries should be addressed to Permissions Department, William Morrow and Company, Inc., 1350 Avenue of the Americas, New York, N.Y. 10019.

It is the policy of William Morrow and Company, Inc., and its imprints and affiliates, recognizing the importance of preserving what has been written, to print the books we publish on acid-free paper, and we exert our best efforts to that end.

Library of Congress Cataloging-in-Publication Data has been applied for.

ISBN 0-688-15991-5

Printed in the United States of America

First Edition

2   3   4   5   6   7   8   9   10

BOOK DESIGN BY JO ANNE METSCH

www.williammorrow.com

Foreword

Not too many years ago, a book like *Quotable Women of the Twentieth Century* would have been deemed unimportant, or not published at all. But a lot has changed over the past century, and the views, opinions, philosophies, and wit of women of this century are of paramount importance. The views of women have, in fact, never been insignificant, but women's ideas have been largely ignored.

Women are in places that a hundred years ago would have been impossible dreams—they are heads of countries, Supreme Court justices, astronauts, and major forces in the entertainment industry. The voices of women are more than just being heard now; they are being heeded. This is what *Quotable Women of the Twentieth Century* is about; the incredible wisdom and insight of women in America and around the world who are shaping our planet's destiny.

In *Quotable Women of the Twentieth Century* you'll hear from heads of state such as Golda Meir: "I can honestly say that I was never affected by the question of the success of an undertaking. If I felt it was the right thing to do, I was for it regardless of the possible outcome." From actors such as Carrie Fisher: "Actors may know how to act, but a lot of them don't know how to behave." And from writers such as Cynthia Ozick: "After a certain number of years, our faces become our biographies."

Some of these quotations are profound or uplifting. Others are insightful or instructive. Many are just fun or funny. Some of these women's thoughts you'll disagree with; others will strike a strong chord with you. But each and every one of the words in *Quotable Women of the Twentieth Century* will have an impact on all of us.

Women have come a long way over the past centuries. Still, women have to fight to attain the same power, position, and respect that many men have. Take the case of Susan Trescher who was recently elected to the all-male board of the Santa Barbara Bancorp company. As a shareholder, Ms. Trescher wanted to see a woman on the company's board: herself. The all-male board refused and Susan Trescher, Harvard Law School graduate, won a position on the board through a proxy vote of the company's stockholders. Women still hold only 10 percent of the board positions in Fortune 500 companies. Women are in the minority in the United States Congress. No woman has been elected president or vice president of the United States. Women athletes, especially those on team sports, have a second-class status to men. Women have difficulty gaining respect—or even jobs—in certain male-dominated fields such as fire fighting.

Indeed, the progress of women has been a long journey. The women's rights movement, originating in the eighteenth century during the Age of Enlightenment in Europe, questioned the stale notions that people's rights were based on their wealth and status. The ideas of this movement helped inspire the American Revolution. For the next century, though, these enlightened ideals did little to foster change in women' s rights in either the United States or in Europe, where a woman's position in society depended primarily on her husband. Yet the seed was planted.

Throughout much of the nineteenth century in both the United States and Europe a woman could not own property in her own name, write a will, or bring a lawsuit. In the 1830s there were several women-only abolitionist movements (women weren't allowed in male abolitionist organizations). Women were fighting on two fronts: to prohibit slavery and to allow antislavery women the same voice the abolitionist men had. These abolitionist crusades later became a driving force for the women's suffrage movement. Property rights were given to women in the United States, with New York leading the way, in 1848. In this country, in part, women's right to vote was an outgrowth of women being active in other social movements.

In the early nineteenth century, large numbers of women joined evangelical groups whose goals were moral and social reforms, including abstinence from alcohol, improvement of the lives of prostitutes, greater employment for women, and increased wages for women. Around the 1850s women began to advocate "voluntary motherhood": a woman could refuse sexual intercourse with her husband if she didn't want to become pregnant. Margaret Sanger and Emma Goldman appeared around the turn of the century and advocated a woman's right to birth control. For writing about this in the magazine called *The Woman Rebel*, Sanger and Goldman were convicted of violating the Comstock Law of 1873, which forbade the mailing of obscene materials across state lines. Anything about birth control was considered obscene. The Comstock Law was finally overturned by a court decision in 1938, which ruled that birth control was not illegal.

Women's rights rarely fared better outside the United States; often they were much worse. In England, in the early nineteenth century, women who were too rebellious (as well as witches and prostitutes) were subjected to the ducking stool. The ducking stool was a seesawlike device that lowered one end—the woman's end—into a river or pond. A magistrate determined how many times the offender was to be lowered into the water. In Great Britain in 1832, middle-class men got to vote for members of Parliament; women over age thirty were given the same right in 1918. Women over the age of twenty-one could vote starting in 1928. In Canada, women were given the right to vote in 1918; in France it was 1944; in Switzerland 1971.

The twentieth century has been a time of incredible change—for the world and for women. Women couldn't vote in the United States until 1920 and couldn't serve on juries. Only in 1963 did it become law in this country that women and men who performed the same work had to be paid the same wage, and women didn't have equal rights in the workplace until 1964. Full equality, proposed through the Equal Rights Amendment to the United States Constitution, was defeated.

Over the past few centuries, women's rights have moved forward on fronts other than those that are economic, political, and legal. Starting in the nineteenth century, reproductive rights become a principle focus of women's rights advocates, but it wasn't until 1973 that the United States Supreme Court ruled that a woman has the right to an abortion.

There are lots of reasons why discrimination against women was so prevalent in the early part of this century and still exists in many forms both here and abroad. To a large degree, male chauvinism still runs strong in the minds of many men. "Chauvinism" comes from the name of a French soldier, Nicolas Chauvin, who continued to brag about Napoleon's victories and prowess even after Napoleon's defeat at Waterloo. People ridiculed Chauvin for his undying veneration of Napoleon—

hence chauvinism became the prejudiced belief in the supe-
riority of one's own group. (Chauvin was popularized in the
play *La Cocarde Tricolore* in 1831.)

It seems incredible today that women's basic political rights
took so long to be realized. In some fields, though, women
were making incredible scientific, medical, and political break-
throughs:

- Caroline Lucretia Herschel discovered three comets and
  eight nebulas in the early 1800s.
- Marie Curie, in the late 1800s, along with her husband,
  discovered the elements radium and polonium and set the
  groundwork for modern physics.
- Dorothy Crawford Hodgkin received the Nobel Prize in
  Chemistry in 1964 for discovering the structure of chem-
  icals used to fight pernicious anemia.
- Geraldine Ferraro became the first woman to be a vice
  presidential candidate of a major political party in 1984.

Chauvinism, bigotry, indifference, false philosophies, and
greed have all played a role in the repression of women. Today women are the leaders of some ten countries; yet in more
than one hundred nations there are no women in the legis-
latures. In the largest thousand non-American companies,
women comprise about 1 percent of the executives and man-
agers.

But out of this repression and gradual realization of women's
basic rights and liberties have come great thoughts and brilliant minds. Not just in politics, but in art, science, literature—
in every endeavor. Woman have had no choice but to be
smart, creative, and expressive, and, most of all, outspoken.
Quotable Women of the Twentieth Century is a book about change—

one that has taken place at a faster rate during this century than at any other time in history. It is more than just a book of quotations; it is a book of the visions, aspirations, and ideas of women from around the world.

CATHLEEN BLACK

Contents

"The next best thing to being clever is being able to quote someone who is."

—MARY PETTIBONE POOLE,
1938

QUOTABLE
WOMEN
OF THE
TWENTIETH
CENTURY

Achievement

One can never consent to creep when one feels an impulse to soar.

HELEN KELLER

The only way to enjoy anything in this life is to earn it first.

GINGER ROGERS

My mother drew a distinction between achievement and success. She said that achievement is the knowledge that you have studied and worked hard and done the best that is in you. Success is being praised by others, and that's nice, too, but not as important or satisfying. Always aim for achievement and forget about success.

HELEN HAYES

If you set out to be liked, you would be prepared to compromise on anything at any time, and you would achieve nothing.

MARGARET THATCHER

Never help a child with a task at which he feels he can succeed.

MARIA MONTESSORI

I used to want the words "She tried" on my tombstone. Now I want "She did it."

KATHERINE DUNHAM

There is only one real sin and that is to persuade oneself that the second best is anything but second best.

DORIS LESSING

Begin somewhere; you cannot build a reputation on what you intend to do.

LIZ SMITH

I can honestly say that I was never affected by the question of the success of an undertaking. If I felt it was the right thing to do, I was for it regardless of the possible outcome.

GOLDA MEIR

None of us suddenly becomes something overnight. The preparations have been in the making for a lifetime.

GAIL GODWIN

The most effective way to do it, is *to do it*.

TONI CADE BAMBARA

Once I decide to do something, I can't have people telling me I can't. If there's a roadblock, you jump over it, walk around it, crawl under it.

KITTY KELLEY

There is a spirit and a need and a man at the beginning of every great human advance. Every one of these must be right for that particular moment of history, or nothing happens.

CORETTA SCOTT KING

I always wanted to be somebody. If I made it, it's half because I was game enough to take a lot of punishment along the way and half because there were a lot of people who cared enough to help me.

ALTHEA GIBSON

If I had one wish for my children, it would be that each of them would reach for goals that have meaning for them as individuals.

LILLIAN CARTER

I can remember walking as a child. It was not customary to say you were fatigued. It was customary to complete the goal of the expedition.

KATHARINE HEPBURN

Acting

Acting is a form of confession.

TALLULAH BANKHEAD

Acting is a matter of giving away secrets.

ELLEN BARKIN

Without wonder and insight, acting is just a trade. With it, it becomes creation.

BETTE DAVIS

Once the curtain is raised, the actor ceases to belong to himself. He belongs to his character, to his author, to his public. He must do the impossible to identify himself with the first, not to betray the second, and not to disappoint the third.

SARAH BERNHARDT

Audiences are the same all over the world, and if you entertain them, they'll respond.

LIZA MINNELLI

Acting is standing up naked and turning around slowly.

ROSALIND RUSSELL

It's such a cuckoo business. And it's a business you go into because you are an egocentric. It's a very embarrassing profession.

KATHARINE HEPBURN

Activism

Science may have found a cure for most evils; but it has found no remedy for the worst of them all—the apathy of human beings.

HELEN KELLER

Everybody wants to do something to help, but nobody wants to be first.

PEARL BAILEY

Nothing liberates our greatness like the desire to help, the desire to serve.

MARIANNE WILLIAMSON

Action is the antidote to despair.

JOAN BAEZ

Never doubt that a small group of thoughtful, committed citizens can change the world. Indeed, it's the only thing that ever has.

MARGARET MEAD

We must not, in trying to think about how we can make a big difference, ignore the small daily differences we can make which, over time, add up to big differences that we often cannot foresee.

MARIAN WRIGHT EDELMAN

We can do no great things—only small things with great love.

MOTHER TERESA

One never notices what has been done; one can only see what remains to be done.

MARIE CURIE

Charity separates the rich from the poor; aid raises the needy and sets him on the same level with the rich.

EVA PERÓN

Until I die, I'm going to keep doing. My people need me. They need somebody that's not taking from them and is giving them something.

CLARA MCBRIDE HALE

Most Americans have never seen the ignorance, degradation, hunger, sickness, and the futility in which many other Americans live. . . . They won't become involved in economic or political change until something brings the seriousness of the situation home to them.

SHIRLEY CHISHOLM

I'm not an American hero. I'm a person who loves children.

CLARA MCBRIDE HALE

You can do one of two things; just shut up, which is something I don't find easy, or learn an awful lot very fast, which is what I tried to do.

JANE FONDA

The more visible signs of protest are gone, but I think there is a realization that the tactics of the late-60s are not sufficient to meet the challenges of the 70s.

CORETTA SCOTT KING

When you're in your 90's and looking back, it's not going to be how much money you made or how many awards you've won. It's really what did you stand for. Did you make a positive difference for people?

ELIZABETH DOLE

Pray for the dead and fight like hell for the living.

MOTHER JONES

It is the duty of youth to bring its fresh new powers to bear on social progress. Each generation of young people should be to the world like a vast reserve force to a tired army. They should lift the world forward. That is what they are for.

CHARLOTTE PERKINS GILMAN

Actors

After my screen test, the director clapped his hands gleefully and yelled, "She can't talk! She can't act! She's sensational!"

AVA GARDNER

I'm tired of playing worn-out depressing ladies in frayed bathrobes. I'm going to get a new hairdo and look terrific and go back to school and even if nobody notices, I'm going to be the most self-fulfilled lady on the block.

JOANNE WOODWARD

Actors may know how to act, but a lot of them don't know how to behave.

CARRIE FISHER

Without discipline and detachment, an actor is an emotional slob, spilling his insides out. This abandonment is having an unfortunate vogue. It is tasteless, formless, absurd. Without containment there is no art. All this vomiting and wheezing and bursting at the seams is no more great acting than the convulsions of raving maniacs.

BETTE DAVIS

Whatever good I have accomplished as an actress I believe came in direct proportion to my efforts to portray black women who have made positive contributions to my heritage.

CICELY TYSON

Make them laugh, make them cry, and back to laughter. What do people go to the theater for? An emotional exercise . . . I am a servant of the people. I have never forgotten that.

MARY PICKFORD

Five stages in the life of an actor . . . 1. Who's Mary Astor? 2. Get me Mary Astor. 3. Get me a Mary Astor type. 4. Get me a young Mary Astor. 5. Who's Mary Astor?

MARY ASTOR

Every actor has a natural animosity toward every other actor, present or absent, living or dead.

LOUISE BROOKS

For an actress to be a success she must have the face of Venus, the brains of Minerva, the grace of Terpsichore, the memory of Macaulay, the figure of Juno, and the hide of a rhinoceros.

ETHEL BARRYMORE

We're harmless megalomaniacs, fanatic in our devotion to a profession which rarely rewards us with a livelihood. Since we court public display we're the foes of privacy. The glass house is our favorite residence.

TALLULAH BANKHEAD

Advice

Advice is one of those things it is far more blessed to give than to receive.

CAROLYN WELLS

I don't give advice. I can't tell anybody what to do. Instead I say this is what we know about this problem at this time. And here are the consequences of these actions.

DR. JOYCE BROTHERS

It is far more impressive when others discover your good qualities without your help.

MISS MANNERS (JUDITH MARTIN)

My motto—*sans limites.*

ISADORA DUNCAN

Don't compromise yourself. You're all you've got.

JANIS JOPLIN

Woman must not accept; she must challenge. She must not be awed by that which has been built up around her; she must revere that woman in her which struggles for expression.

MARGARET SANGER

It's totally okay to be a normie.

DREW BARRYMORE

Advice is what we ask for when we already know the answer but wish we didn't.

ERICA JONG

Never face facts; if you do you'll never get up in the morning.

MARLO THOMAS

You must learn to be still in the midst of activity, and to be vibrantly alive in repose.

INDIRA GANDHI

To wear your heart on your sleeve isn't a very good plan; you should wear it inside, where it functions best.

MARGARET THATCHER

When in doubt, make a fool of yourself. There is a microscopically thin line between being brilliantly creative and acting like the most gigantic idiot on earth. So what the hell, leap!

CYNTHIA HEIMEL

This is the gist of what I know:
Give advice and buy a foe.

PHYLLIS MCGINLEY

Worry less about what other people think about you, and more about what you think of them.

FAY WELDON

Everybody knows if you are too careful you are so occupied in being careful that you are sure to stumble over something.

GERTRUDE STEIN

Follow your instincts. That's where true wisdom manifests itself.

OPRAH WINFREY

Risk! Risk anything! Care no more for the opinions of others, for those voices. Do the hardest thing on earth for you. Act for yourself. Face the truth.

KATHERINE MANSFIELD

And the trouble is, if you don't risk anything, you risk even more.

ERICA JONG

Age/Aging

The hardest years in life are those between ten and seventy.

HELEN HAYES

After a certain number of years, our faces become our biographies.

CYNTHIA OZICK

Every age can be enchanting, provided you live within it.

BRIGITTE BARDOT

We are the same people as we were at three, six, ten or twenty years old. More noticeably so, perhaps, at six or seven, because we were not pretending so much then.

AGATHA CHRISTIE

The really frightening thing about middle age is the knowledge that you'll grow out of it.

DORIS DAY

Perhaps one has to be very old before one learns how to be amused rather than shocked.

PEARL S. BUCK

I refuse to admit that I am more than fifty-two, even if that does make my sons illegitimate.

NANCY ASTOR

Youth is something very new: twenty years ago no one mentioned it.

COCO CHANEL

There are no old people nowadays; they are either "wonderful for their age" or dead.

MARY PETTIBONE POOLE

Old age is when the liver spots show through your gloves.

PHYLLIS DILLER

I used to dread getting older because I thought I would not be able to do all the things I wanted to do, but now that I am older I find that I don't want to do them.

LADY NANCY ASTOR

Discussing how old you are is the temple of boredom.

RUTH GORDON

I have no romantic feelings about age. Either you are interesting at any age or you are not. There is nothing particularly interesting about being old—or being young, for that matter.

KATHARINE HEPBURN

Old age is like a plane flying through a storm. Once you are aboard there is nothing you can do.

GOLDA MEIR

I believe the true function of age is memory. I'm recording as fast as I can.

RITA MAE BROWN

One of the many things nobody ever tells you about middle age is that it's such a nice change from being young.

DOROTHY CANFIELD FISHER

We are always the same age inside.

GERTRUDE STEIN

Old age is no place for sissies.

BETTE DAVIS

Age is something that doesn't matter, unless you are a cheese.

BILLIE BURKE

There *is* a fountain of youth: It is your mind, your talents, the creativity you bring to your life and the lives of people you love. When you learn to tap this source, you will truly have defeated age.

SOPHIA LOREN

For inside all the weakness of old age, the spirit, God knows, is as mercurial as it ever was.

MAY SARTON

As I grow older, part of my emotional survival plan must be to actively seek inspiration instead of passively waiting for it to find me.

BEBE MOORE CAMPBELL

A woman may develop wrinkles and cellulite, lose her waistline, her bustline, her ability to bear a child, even her sense of humor, but none of that implies a loss of her sexuality, her femininity.

BARBARA GORDON

Being over seventy is like being engaged in a war. All of our friends are going or gone and we survive amongst the dead and dying as on a battlefield.

MURIEL SPARK

Careful grooming may take twenty years off a woman's age, but you can't fool a long flight of stairs.

MARLENE DIETRICH

The lovely thing about being forty is that you can appreciate twenty-five-year-old men.

COLLEEN MCCULLOUGH

To be somebody you must last.

RUTH GORDON

I have everything I had twenty years ago, only it's a little bit slower.

GYPSY ROSE LEE

The secret of staying younger is to live honestly, eat slowly, and lie about your age.

LUCILLE BALL

It is sad to grow old but nice to ripen.

BRIGITTE BARDOT

Another belief of mine: that everyone else my age is an adult, whereas I am merely in disguise.

MARGARET ATWOOD

From birth to age eighteen, a girl needs good parents. From eighteen to thirty-five, she needs good looks. From thirty-five to fifty-five, she needs a good personality. From fifty-five on, she needs good cash.

SOPHIE TUCKER

Alcohol

People who drink to drown their sorrow should be told that sorrow knows how to swim.

ANN LANDERS

When a woman drinks it's as if an animal were drinking, or a child. Alcoholism is scandalous in a woman, and a female alcoholic is rare, a serious matter. It's a slur on the divine in our nature.

MARGUERITE DURAS

Even though a number of people have tried, no one has yet found a way to drink for a living.

JEAN KERR

One reason I don't drink is that I want to know when I'm having a good time.

NANCY ASTOR

The less I behave like Whistler's mother the night before, the more I look like her the morning after.

TALLULAH BANKHEAD

Alcohol doesn't console, it doesn't fill up anyone's psychological gaps, all it replaces is the lack of God. It doesn't comfort man. On the contrary, it encourages him in his folly, it transports him to the supreme regions where he is the master of his own destiny.

MARGUERITE DURAS

Unrecognized alcoholism is the ruling pathology among writers and intellectuals.

DIANA TRILLING

Do not allow your children to mix drinks. It is unseemly and they use too much vermouth.

FRAN LEBOWITZ

Ambition

If God lets me live, I shall attain more than Mummy ever has done, I shall not remain insignificant, shall work in the world and for mankind!

ANNE FRANK

I've always tried to go a step past wherever people expected me to end up.

BEVERLY SILLS

If ambition doesn't hurt you, you haven't got it.

KATHLEEN NORRIS

I had to make my own living and my own opportunity. . . . Don't sit down and wait for the opportunities to come; you have to get up and make them.

MADAME C. J. WALKER

There is no point at which you can say, "Well, I'm successful now. I might as well take a nap."

CARRIE FISHER

Far away there in the sunshine are my highest aspirations. I may not reach them, but I can look up and see their beauty, believe in them, and try to follow where they lead.

LOUISA MAY ALCOTT

I have the same goal I've had ever since I was a little girl. I want to rule the world.

MADONNA

I do want to get rich but I never want to do what there is to do to get rich.

GERTRUDE STEIN

Ambition if it feeds at all, does so on the ambition of others.

SUSAN SONTAG

Art

Art is a wicked thing. It is what we are.

GEORGIA O'KEEFFE

Contemporary art, no matter how much it has defined itself by a taste for negation, can still be analyzed as a set of assertions of a formal kind.

SUSAN SONTAG

Art is not living. It is the use of living.

AUDRE LORDE

Art, it seems to me, should simplify.

WILLA CATHER

Art and religion first; then philosophy; lastly science. That is the order of the great subjects of life, their order of importance.

MURIEL SPARK

Art is the only way to run away without leaving home.

TWYLA THARP

In the first grade, I already knew the pattern of my life. I didn't know the living of it, but I knew the line. . . . From the first day in school until the day I graduated, everyone gave me one hundred plus in art. Well, where do you go in life? You go to the place where you got one hundred plus.

LOUISE NEVELSON

What would life be without art? Science prolongs life. To consist of what—eating, drinking, and sleeping? What is the good of living longer if it is only a matter of satisfying the requirements that sustain life? All this is nothing without the charm of art.

SARAH BERNHARDT

I felt a comedy ego beginning to grow, which gave me the courage to begin tentatively looking into myself for material.

JOAN RIVERS

A work of art is one through which the consciousness of the artist is able to give its emotions to anyone who is prepared to receive them. There is no such thing as bad art.

MURIEL RUKEYSER

Art is the only thing that can go on mattering once it has stopped hurting.

ELIZABETH BOWEN

Religion and art spring from the same root and are close kin. Economics and art are strangers.

WILLA CATHER

Art is a form of catharsis.

DOROTHY PARKER

Art is not for the cultivated taste. It is to cultivate taste.

NIKKI GIOVANNI

Artists

The artist . . . is the voice of the people.

ALICE WALKER

Artists were intended to be an ornament to society. As a society in themselves they are unthinkable.

ELIZABETH BOWEN

The most potent and sacred command which can be laid upon any artist is the command: wait.

IRIS MURDOCH

Trouble is said to be good for an artist's soul but almost never is.

RITA MAE BROWN

If I didn't start painting, I would have raised chickens.

GRANDMA MOSES

The cynicism of the young about society is as nothing to the cynicism of young artists of the art establishment.

NANCY HALE

The painter . . . does not fit the paints to the world. He most certainly does not fit the world to himself. He fits himself to the paint. The self is the servant who bears the paintbox and its inherited contents.

ANNIE DILLARD

To reproach artists for having an insufficiently radical relation to the world has to be a complaint about art as such. And to reproach art is, in more than one way, like reproaching consciousness itself for being a burden.

SUSAN SONTAG

Athletes

People don't pay much attention to you when you are second best. I wanted to see what it felt like to be number one.

FLORENCE GRIFFITH JOYNER

I like to laugh, but on the court, it is my work. I try to smile, but it is so difficult. I concentrate on the ball, not on my face.

STEFFI GRAF

I don't think being an athlete is unfeminine. I think of it as a kind of grace.

JACKIE JOYNER-KERSEE

It doesn't matter what anybody thinks of what I do. The clock doesn't lie.

BONNIE BLAIR

I think I look good out there. I'm strong, powerful, and artistic. But I have my doubts as much as anyone. And there are so many more things to life than skating—I hope.

JILL TRENARY

Every problem in your life goes away in front of a bull. Because *this* problem, the bull, is bigger than all other problems. Of course I have fear, but it is fear that I will fail the responsibility I have taken on in front of all those people—not fear of the bull. Death becomes unimportant when I am in front of him. I feel so good, it does not matter if he kills me.

CRISTINA SANCHEZ
ON BULLFIGHTING

Beauty

When you've got the personality, you don't need the nudity.

MAE WEST

What is most beautiful in virile men is something feminine; what is most beautiful in feminine women is something masculine.

SUSAN SONTAG

The truth, the absolute truth, is that the chief beauty for the theater consists in fine bodily proportions.

SARAH BERNHARDT

People see you as an object, not as a person, and they project a set of expectations onto you. People who don't have it think beauty is a blessing, but actually it sets you apart.

CANDICE BERGEN

Circumstances alter faces.

CAROLYN WELLS

Although they tell you you are most beautiful when you're pregnant, all the models who epitomize beauty have skinny waistlines. So they're shitting you right from the start.

FLORYNCE KENNEDY

If you see someone with a stunning haircut, grab her by the wrist and demand fiercely to know the name, address, and home phone number of her hairdresser. If she refuses to tell you, burst into tears.

CYNTHIA HEIMEL

My gift is that I'm not beautiful. My career was never about looks. It's about health and being in good shape.

SHIRLEY MACLAINE

Everything you see I owe to spaghetti.

SOPHIA LOREN

When I go to the beauty parlor, I always use the emergency entrance. Sometimes I just go for an estimate.

PHYLLIS DILLER

I think women see me on the cover of magazines and think I never have a pimple or bags under my eyes. You have to realize that's after two hours of hair and makeup, plus retouching. Even *I* don't wake up looking like Cindy Crawford.

CINDY CRAWFORD

It is very fashionable for good-looking ladies to say how hard it is to be beautiful, but that's not true. There are times when it depresses and bothers me to see just how easy things are made for a beautiful woman.

CATHERINE DENEUVE

Plain women know more about men than beautiful ones do.

KATHARINE HEPBURN

Anybody who thinks that society pressures women to live up to our image should think of what we have to go through to maintain that image.

CAROL ALT

All God's children are not beautiful. Most of God's children are, in fact, barely presentable.

FRAN LEBOWITZ

For a long time the only time I felt beautiful—in the sense of being complete as a woman, as a human being, and even female—was when I was singing.

LEONTYNE PRICE

The beauty industry helped to deepen the psychic isolation that so many women felt in the 80s, by reinforcing the representation of women's problems as purely personal ills, unrelated to social pressures and curable only to the degree that the individual woman succeeded in fitting the universal standard—by physically changing herself.

SUSAN FALUDI

We know that every woman wants to be thin. Our images of womanhood are almost synonymous with thinness.

SUSIE ORBACH

A woman obsessed with her body is also obsessed with the limitations of her emotional life.

KIM CHERNIN

Beauty is everlasting
and dust is for a time.

MARIANNE MOORE

I'm tired of all this nonsense about beauty being only skin-deep. That's deep enough. What do you want, an adorable pancreas?

JEAN KERR

I argue that we deserve the choice to do whatever we want with our faces and bodies without being punished by an ideology that is using attitudes, economic pressure, and even legal judgments regarding women's appearance to undermine us psychologically and politically.

NAOMI WOLF

Taking joy in life is a woman's best cosmetic.

ROSALIND RUSSELL

Long tresses down to the floor can be beautiful, if you have that, but learn to love what you have.

ANITA BAKER

As far as beauty is concerned, in order to be confident we must accept that the way we look and feel is our own responsibility.

SOPHIA LOREN

To regain a healthy sense of self-worth I first had to break down old fears and doubts and anxieties. Only then was I able to reshape my images successfully. Now, my exterior and interior are in harmony. I really feel as good as I look. And dammit, I know I look good.

ELIZABETH TAYLOR

I base most of my fashion taste on what doesn't itch.

GILDA RADNER

The average man is more interested in a woman who is interested in him than he is in a woman—any woman—with beautiful legs.

MARLENE DIETRICH

You can't be too rich or too thin.

WALLIS SIMPSON,
DUCHESS OF WINDSOR

Belief

To have a reason to get up in the morning, it is necessary to possess a guiding principle. A belief of some kind. A bumper sticker if you will.

JUDITH GUEST

The trouble is that not enough people have come together with the firm determination to live the things which they say they believe.

ELEANOR ROOSEVELT

To believe in something not yet proved and to underwrite it with our lives; it is the only way we can leave the future open.

LILLIAN SMITH

There are no atheists on turbulent airplanes.

ERICA JONG

They were so strong in their beliefs that there came a time when it hardly mattered what exactly those beliefs were; they all fused into a single stubbornness.

LOUISE ERDRICH

Not seeing is half-believing.

VITA SACKVILLE-WEST

Birth Control

Only a controlled fertility in human beings can maintain any progress. No system of society depending for its continuation on intelligent humans can stand long unless it encourages the control of the birth rate and includes contraceptive knowledge as a right. Without it no system, no matter what its ideals, can withstand the overpowering force of uncontrolled, unrestricted fecundity.

MARGARET SANGER

Given a choice between hearing my daughter say "I'm pregnant" or "I used a condom," most mothers would get up in the middle of the night and buy them herself.

JOYCELYN ELDERS

No woman can call herself free who does not own and control her body. No woman can call herself free until she can choose consciously whether she will or will not be a mother.

MARGARET SANGER

The greatest of all contraceptives is affluence.

INDIRA GANDHI

If we can get that realistic feminine morality working for us, if we can trust ourselves and so let women think and feel that an unwanted child or an oversize family is wrong—not ethically wrong, not against the rules, but morally wrong, all wrong, wrong like a thalidomide birth, wrong like taking a wrong step that will break your neck—if we can get feminine and human morality out from under the yoke of a dead ethic, then maybe we'll begin to get somewhere on the road that leads to survival.

URSULA K. LE GUIN

Books

Until I feared I would lose it, I never loved to read. One does not love breathing.

HARPER LEE

Books, books, books. It was not that I read so much. I read and reread the same ones. But all of them were necessary to me. Their presence, their smell, the letters of their titles, and the texture of their leather bindings.

COLETTE

All books are either dreams or swords.

AMY LOWELL

It had been startling and disappointing to me to find out that story books had been written by *people*, that books were not natural wonders, coming up of themselves like grass. Yet regardless of where they came from, I cannot remember a time when I was not in love with them—with the books themselves, cover and binding and the paper they were printed on, with their smell and their weight and with their possession in my arms, capture and carried off to myself. Still illiterate, I was ready for them, committed to all the reading I could give them.

EUDORA WELTY

Life-transforming ideas have always come to me through books.

BELL HOOKS

My home is where my books are.

ELLEN THOMPSON

I hoard books. They are people who do not leave.

ANNE SEXTON

If I read a book that impresses me, I have to take myself firmly in hand, before I mix with other people; otherwise they would think my mind rather queer.

ANNE FRANK

I believe I belong to the last literary generation, the last generation, that is, for whom books are a religion.

ERICA JONG

I have decided that the trouble with print is, it never changes its mind.

URSULA K. LE GUIN

Bureaucracy

Bureaucracy, the rule of no one, has become the modern form of despotism.

MARY MCCARTHY

No civilization . . . would ever have been possible without a framework of stability, to provide the wherein for the flux of change. Foremost among the stabilizing factors, more enduring than customs, manners and traditions, are the legal systems that regulate our life in the world and our daily affairs with each other.

HANNAH ARENDT

I'm sorry that government involves filling out a lot of forms . . . I'm sorry myself that we're not still on the frontier, where we could all tote guns, shoot anything that moved and spit to our hearts' content. But we live in a diverse and crowded country, and with civilization comes regulation.

MOLLY IVINS

The speed with which bureaucracy has invaded almost every branch of human activity is something astounding once one thinks about it.

SIMONE WEIL

It seems to me that there must be an ecological limit to the number of paper pushers the earth can sustain, and that human civilization will collapse when the number of, say, tax lawyers exceeds the world's population of farmers, weavers, fisherpersons, and pediatric nurses.

BARBARA EHRENREICH

It never pays to deal with the flyweights of the world. They take far too much pleasure in thwarting you at every turn.

SUE GRAFTON

What gets me is you work all your life like a dog, you pay into these government programs. But still, when you need help, the people that's paid to help you they act like it's coming out of their own pocket.

ARTIE CHANDLER

Business

Dear, never forget one little point: It's my business. You just work here.

ELIZABETH ARDEN TO HER HUSBAND

If you put a woman in a man's position, she will be more efficient, but no more kind.

FAY WELDON

The trouble with the rat race is that even if you win you're still a rat.

LILY TOMLIN

If women can sleep their way to the top, how come they aren't there? . . . There must be an epidemic of insomnia out there.

ELLEN GOODMAN

Business was his aversion; pleasure was his business.

MARIA EDGEWORTH

The more important the title, the more self-important the person, the greater the amount of time spent on the Eastern shuttle, the more suspicious the man and the less vitality in the organization.

JANE O'REILLY

This morning I threw up at a board meeting. I was sure the cat was out of the bag, but no one seemed to think anything about it; apparently it's quite common for people to throw up at board meetings.

JANE WAGNER

Capital Punishment

Something in me has always been opposed to capital punishment. What right has one group of human beings to take away the life of any other human being?

ELEANOR ROOSEVELT

As a Christian, as an individual, as a doctor, I am absolutely opposed to the death penalty.

JOYCELYN ELDERS

I hope to die at my post: in the streets or in prison.

ROSA LUXEMBURG
IN LETTER FROM PRISON

I believe that people would be alive today if there were a death penalty.

NANCY REAGAN

People are more than the worst thing they have ever done in their lives.

HELEN PREJEAN

Censorship

If a man is pictured chopping off a woman's breast, it only gets an R rating; but if, God forbid, a man is pictured kissing a woman's breast, it gets an X rating. Why is violence more acceptable than tenderness?

SALLY STRUTHERS

Literature is one of the few areas left where black and white feel some identity of purpose; we all struggle under censorship.

NADINE GORDIMER

Censorship, like charity, should begin at home; but unlike charity, it should end there.

CLARE BOOTHE LUCE

God forbid that any book should be banned. The practice is as indefensible as infanticide.

REBECCA WEST

One thing is sure—none of the arts flourishes on censorship and repression. And by this time it should be evident that the American public is capable of doing its own censoring.

ELEANOR ROOSEVELT

I believe in censorship. After all, I made a fortune out of it.

MAE WEST

Censorship is never over for those who have experienced it. It is a brand on the imagination that affects the individual who has suffered it.

NADINE GORDIMER

Challenges

For me life is a challenge. And it will be a challenge if I live to be a hundred or if I get to be a trillionaire.

BEAH RICHARDS

You gain strength, courage and confidence by every experience which you must stop and look fear in the face. . . . You must do the thing you think you cannot do.

ELEANOR ROOSEVELT

To be tested is good. The challenged life may be the best therapist.

GAIL SHEEHY

For me it's the challenge—the challenge to try to beat myself or do better than I did in the past. I try to keep in mind not what I have accomplished but what I have to try to accomplish in the future.

JACKIE JOYNER-KERSEE

Please know that I am aware of the hazards. I want to do it because I want to do it. Women must try to do things as men have tried. When they fail, their failure must be a challenge to others.

AMELIA EARHART

When people keep telling you that you can't do a thing, you kind of like to try it.

MARGARET CHASE SMITH

Change

You must change in order to survive.

PEARL BAILEY

The moment of change is the only poem.

ADRIENNE RICH

The challenges of change are always hard. It is important that we begin to unpack those challenges that confront this nation and realize that we each have a role that requires us to change and become more responsible for shaping our own future.

HILLARY RODHAM CLINTON

People change and forget to tell each other.

LILLIAN HELLMAN

The need for change bulldozed a road down the center of my mind.

MAYA ANGELOU

My parents were always philosophizing about how to bring about change. To me, people who didn't try to make the world a better place were strange.

CAROL MOSELEY BRAUN

Changes are not only possible and predictable, but to deny them is to be an accomplice to one's own necessary vegetation.

GAIL SHEEHY

Childhood

When it comes time to do your own life, you either perpetuate your childhood or you stand on it and finally kick it out from under.

ROSELLEN BROWN

Childhood is not from birth to a certain age and at
  a certain age
The child is grown, and puts away childish things.
Childhood is the kingdom where nobody dies.

EDNA ST. VINCENT MILLAY

What we forget as children is that our parents are children, also. The child in them has not been satisfied or met or loved, often. Not always, but very often. Oftener, actually, than is admitted.

EDNA O'BRIEN

What we remember from childhood we remember forever— permanent ghosts, stamped, imprinted, eternally seen.

CYNTHIA OZICK

The ability to forget a sorrow is childhood's most enchanting feature.

PHYLLIS MCGINLEY

When I was born I was so surprised I didn't talk for a year and half.

GRACIE ALLEN

Little girls are cute and small only to adults. To one another they are not cute. They are life-sized.

MARGARET ATWOOD

Children

The legacy I want to leave is a child-care system that says that no kid is going to be left alone or left unsafe.

MARIAN WRIGHT EDELMAN

Don't forget that compared to a grownup person every baby is a genius. Think of the capacity to learn! The freshness, the temperament, the will of a baby a few months old!

MAY SARTON

Children are forced to live very rapidly in order to live at all. They are given only a few years in which to learn hundreds of thousands of things about life and the planet and themselves.

PHYLLIS MCGINLEY

Children are quite different—mentally, physically, spiritually, quantitatively; and, furthermore, they're all a bit nuts.

JEAN KERR

Cuteness in children is totally an adult perspective. The children themselves are unaware that the quality exists, let alone its desirability, until the reactions of grownups inform them.

LEONTINE YOUNG

[Miss Manners has] been known to make deals with babies, such as "Give me five more minutes' sleep, just five minutes, and I promise you that I'll pick you up and bounce you around again," even though her experience with babies' integrity about fulfilling their sides of the bargains has been disillusioning.

JUDITH MARTIN (MISS MANNERS)

Let our children grow tall, and some taller than others if they have it in them to do so.

MARGARET THATCHER

A child's world is fresh and new and beautiful, full of wonder and excitement. It is our misfortune that for most of us that clear-eyed vision, that true instinct for what is beautiful and awe-inspiring, is dimmed and even lost before we reach adulthood.

RACHEL CARSON

I will never understand children. I never pretended to. I meet mothers all the time who make resolutions to themselves. "I'm going to . . . go out of my way to show them I am interested in them and what they do. I am going to understand my children." These women end up making rag rugs, using blunt scissors.

ERMA BOMBECK

Thank God kids never mean well.

LILY TOMLIN

While admitting that adults frequently make unfortunate remarks to babies, it has to be said that babies, too, can make mistakes.

JEAN KERR

Competition

Competition can damage self-esteem, create anxiety, and lead to cheating and hurt feelings. But so can romantic love.

MARIAH BURTON NELSON

The next best thing to winning is losing! At least you've been in the race.

NELLIE HERSHEY SMITH

Competition is easier to accept if you realize it is not an act of oppression or abrasion. . . . I've worked with my best friends in direct competition.

DIANE SAWYER

You've got to take the initiative and play your game. . . . Confidence makes the difference.

CHRIS EVERT

Whoever said, "It's not whether you win or lose that counts," probably lost.

MARTINA NAVRATILOVA

All of my life I've always had the urge to do things better than anybody else.

BABE DIDRIKSON ZAHARIAS

If you can react the same way to winning and losing, that . . . quality is important because it stays with you the rest of your life.

CHRIS EVERT

Consumerism

It is true that America produces and consumes more cars, soap, and bathtubs than any other nation, but we live among these objects rather than by them.

MARY MCCARTHY

In a capitalist society a man is expected to be an aggressive, uncompromising, factual, lusty, intelligent provider of goods, and the woman, a retiring, gracious, emotional, intuitive, attractive consumer of goods.

TONI CADE BAMBARA

An honest man is one who knows that he can't consume more than he has produced.

AYN RAND

In department stores, so much kitchen equipment is bought indiscriminately by people who just come in for men's underwear.

JULIA CHILD

One quarter of what you buy will turn out to be mistakes.

DELIA EPHRON

America is a consumer culture, and when we change what we buy—and how we buy it—we'll change who we are.

FAITH POPCORN

Conversation/Communication

The opposite of talking isn't listening. The opposite of talking is waiting.

FRAN LEBOWITZ

Talk uses up ideas. . . . Once I have spoken them aloud, they are lost to me, dissipated into the noisy air like smoke. Only if I bury them, like bulbs, in the rich soil of silence do they grow.

DORIS GRUMBACH

Kind words can be short and easy to speak, but their echoes are truly endless.

MOTHER TERESA

Concepts antedate facts.

CHARLOTTE PERKINS GILMAN

The random talk of people who have no chance of immortality and thus can speak their minds out has a setting, often, of lights, streets, houses, human beings, beautiful or grotesque, which will weave itself into the moment forever.

VIRGINIA WOOLF

Nothing could bother me more than the way a thing goes dead once it has been said.

GERTRUDE STEIN

Communication is a continual balancing act, juggling the conflicting needs for intimacy and independence. To survive in the world, we have to act in concert with others, but to survive as ourselves, rather than simply as cogs in a wheel, we have to act alone.

DEBORAH TANNEN

I never know how much of what I say is true.

BETTE MIDLER

The whole art of life is knowing the right time to say things.

MAEVE BINCHY

I have come to believe over and over again that what is most important to me must be spoken, made verbal and shared, even at the risk of having it bruised or misunderstood. That the speaking profits me, beyond any other effect.

AUDRE LORDE

Each person has a literature inside them. But when people lose language, when they have to experiment with putting their thoughts together on the spot—that's what I love most. That's where character lives.

ANNA DEAVERE SMITH

When you stop talking, you've lost your customer.

ESTÉE LAUDER

No one really listens to anyone else, and if you try it for a while you'll see why.

MIGNON MCLAUGHLIN

Brevity is the soul of lingerie.

DOROTHY PARKER

Good communication is stimulating as black coffee, and just as hard to sleep after.

ANNE MORROW LINDBERGH

Don't confuse being stimulating with being blunt.

BARBARA WALTERS

Cooking

To be a good cook you have to have a love of the good, a love of hand work, and a love of creating. Some people like to paint pictures, or do gardening, or build a boat in the basement. Other people get a tremendous pleasure out of the kitchen, because cooking is just as creative and imaginative an activity as drawing, or wood carving, or music. And cooking draws upon your every talent—science, mathematics, energy, history, experience—and the more experience you have the less likely are your experiments to end in drivel and disaster. The more you know, the more you can create. There's no end to imagination in the kitchen.

JULIA CHILD

Architecture might be more sportive and varied if every man built his own house, but it would not be the art and science that we have made it; and while every woman prepares food for her own family, cooking can never rise beyond the level of the amateur's work.

CHARLOTTE PERKINS GILMAN

Life is too short to stuff a mushroom.

SHIRLEY CONRAN

Couples who cook together stay together. (Maybe because they can't decide who'll get the Cuisinart.)

ERICA JONG

I tell people all the time, you have to be in love with that pot. You have to put all your love in that pot. If you're in a hurry, just eat your sandwich and go. Don't even start cooking, because you can't do anything well in a hurry. I love food. I love serving people. I love satisfying people.

CHEF LEAH CHASE

Courage

Courage is very important. Like a muscle, it is strengthened by use.

RUTH GORDON

If you can keep your head when all about are losing theirs, it's just possible you haven't grasped the situation.

JEAN KERR

One isn't necessarily born with courage, but one is born with potential. Without courage, we cannot practice any other virtue with consistency. We can't be kind, true, merciful, generous, or honest.

MAYA ANGELOU

One of the marks of a gift is to have the courage of it (also the talent).

KATHERINE ANNE PORTER

If you are brave too often, people will come to expect it of you.

MIGNON MCLAUGHLIN

It isn't for the moment you are stuck that you need courage, but for the long uphill climb back to sanity and faith and security.

ANNE MORROW LINDBERGH

All serious daring starts from within.

EUDORA WELTY

Life shrinks or expands in proportion to one's courage.

ANAÏS NIN

Courage is the price that life exacts for granting peace. The soul that knows it not, knows no release from little things.

AMELIA EARHART

I became more courageous by doing the very things I needed to be courageous for—first, a little, and badly. Then, bit by bit, more and better. Being avidly—sometimes annoyingly—curious and persistent about discovery how others were doing what I wanted to do.

AUDRE LORDE

Creativity

We are traditionally rather proud of ourselves for having slipped creative work in there between the domestic chores and obligations. I'm not sure we deserve such big A-pluses for all that.

TONI MORRISON

Exchange is creation.

MURIEL RUKEYSER

Woman is frequently praised as the more "creative" sex. She does not need to make poems, it is argued; she has no drive to make poems, because she is privileged to make babies. A pregnancy is as fulfilling as, say, Yeats's "Sailing to Byzantium" . . . To call a child a poem may be a pretty metaphor, but it is a slur on the labor of art.

CYNTHIA OZICK

It takes great passion and great energy to do anything creative, especially in the theater. You have to care so much that you can't sleep, you can't eat, you can't talk to people. It's just got to be right. You can't do it without that passion.

AGNES DE MILLE

Women's art, though created in solitude, wells up out of community. There is, clearly, both enormous hunger for the work thus being diffused, and an explosion of creative energy, bursting through the coercive choicelessness of the system on whose boundaries we are working.

ADRIENNE RICH

Make-believe colors the past with innocent distortion, and it swirls ahead of us in a thousand ways—in science, in politics, in every bold intention. It is part of our collective lives, entwining our past and our future . . . a particularly rewarding aspect of life itself.

SHIRLEY TEMPLE BLACK

Just don't give up trying to do what you really want to do. Where there is love and inspiration, I don't think you can go wrong.

ELLA FITZGERALD

Creative minds have always been known to survive any kind of bad training.

ANNA FREUD

Only when men are connected to large, universal goals are they really happy—and one result of their happiness is a rush of creative activity.

JOYCE CAROL OATES

Crime

No punishment has ever possessed enough power of deterrence to prevent the commission of crimes. On the contrary, whatever the punishment, once a specific crime has appeared for the first time, its reappearance is more likely than its initial emergence could ever have been.

HANNAH ARENDT

Crime is naught but misdirected energy. So long as every institution of today, economic, political, social, and moral, conspires to misdirect human energy into wrong channels; so long as most people are out of place doing the things they hate to do, living a life they loathe to live, crime will be inevitable.

EMMA GOLDMAN

Crime seems to change character when it crosses a bridge or a tunnel. In the city, crime is taken as emblematic of class and race. In the suburbs, though, it's intimate and psychological—resistant to generalization, a mystery of the individual soul.

BARBARA EHRENREICH

We make our own criminals, and their crimes are congruent with the national culture we all share. It has been said that a people get the kind of political leadership they deserve. I think they also get the kinds of crime and criminals they themselves bring into being.

MARGARET MEAD

Lawlessness is a self-perpetuating, ever-expanding habit.

DOROTHY THOMPSON

Crime . . . can be a way of establishing identity or acquiring security—at least the magistrate addresses you by name.

DIANA NORMAN

Stories of law violations are weighed on a different set of scales in the black mind than in the white. Petty crimes embarrass the community and many people wistfully wonder why negroes don't rob more banks, embezzle more funds, and employ more graft in the unions . . . [This] appeals particularly to one who is unable to compete legally with his fellow citizens.

MAYA ANGELOU

Never say anything on the phone that you wouldn't want your mother to hear at your trial.

SYDNEY BIDDLE BARROWS

Critics/Criticism

Unless criticism refuses to take itself quite so seriously or at least to permit its readers not to, it will inevitably continue to reflect the finicky canons of the genteel tradition and the depressing pieties of the Culture Religion of Modernism.

LESLIE FIELDER

A critic is someone who never actually goes to the battle, yet who afterwards comes out shooting the wounded.

TYNE DALY

Criticism . . . makes very little dent upon me, unless I think there is some real justification and something should be done.

ELEANOR ROOSEVELT

Confronted by an absolutely infuriating review, it is sometimes helpful for the victim to do a little personal research on the critic. Is there any truth to the rumor that he had no formal education beyond the age of eleven? In any event, is he able to construct a simple English sentence? Do his participles dangle? When moved to lyricism, doe he write "I had a fun time"? Was he ever arrested for burglary? I don't know that you will prove anything this way, but it is perfectly harmless and quite soothing.

JEAN KERR

Any critic is entitled to wrong judgments, of course. But certain lapses of judgment indicate the radical failure of an entire sensibility.

SUSAN SONTAG

It is healthier, in any case, to write for the adults one's children will become than for the children one's "mature" critics often are.

ALICE WALKER

The greatest honor that can be paid to the work of art, on its pedestal of ritual display, is to *describe* it with sensory completeness. We need a science of description. . . . Criticism is ceremonial revivification.

CAMILLE PAGLIA

Dance

Dance is the landscape of man's soul.

MARTHA GRAHAM

Dance is bigger than the physical body. . . . When you extend your arm, it doesn't stop at the end of your fingers, because you're dancing bigger than that; you're dancing spirit.

JUDITH JAMISON

The truest expression of a people is in its dances and its music.

AGNES DE MILLE

My art is just an effort to express the truth of my being in gesture and movement. It has taken me long years to find even one absolutely true movement.

ISADORA DUNCAN

There are short-cuts to happiness, and dancing is one of them.

VICKI BAUM

A good education is usually harmful to a dancer. A good calf is better than a good head.

AGNES DE MILLE

Part of the joy of dancing is conversation. Trouble is, some men can't talk and dance at the same time.

GINGER ROGERS

The future of dance? If I knew, I'd want to do it first.

MARTHA GRAHAM

I loved dancing with a delirious "I wish I could die" passion . . . but alas! Only one in ten partners had any notion of time, and what made it worse, the nine were always behind, never before the beat. . . . Sometimes I would firmly seize smaller, lighter partners by the scruff of the neck, so to speak, and whirl them along in the way they should go, but I saw they were not enjoying themselves.

ETHEL SMYTH

Death

People die, no matter how much they are needed. It is possible to live and make effective use of one's life, no matter how little one may be personally interested in living.

BERNADETTE DEVLIN

There is in every one of us an unending see-saw between the will to live and the will to die.

REBECCA WEST

I happen to think that a belief in God is all that is necessary for the acceptance of death, since you know that death, like life, is part of God's pattern.

ELEANOR ROOSEVELT

I am incapable of conceiving infinity, and yet I do not accept finity. I want this adventure that is the context of my life to go on without end.

SIMONE DE BEAUVOIR

Death is the last enemy: once we've got past that I think everything will be alright.

ALICE THOMAS ELLIS

While others may argue about whether the world ends with a bang or a whimper, I just want to make sure mine doesn't end with a whine.

BARBARA GORDON

I postpone death by living, by suffering, by error, by risking, by giving, by loving.

ANAÏS NIN

Dying
Is an art, like everything else.
I do it exceptionally well
I do it so it feels like hell.
I do it so it feels real.
I guess you could say I've a call.

SYLVIA PLATH

I think we should look forward to death more than we do. Of course everybody hates to go to bed or miss anything but dying is really the only chance we'll get to rest.

FLORYNCE KENNEDY

I always say my God will take care of me. If it's my time I'll go, and if it's not I won't. I feel that He really has a lot of important things for me to do. And He's going to make sure that I'm here to do them.

JOYCELYN ELDERS

For those who live neither with religious consolations about death nor with a sense of death (or of anything else) as natural, death is the obscene mystery, the ultimate affront, the thing that cannot be controlled. It can only be denied.

SUSAN SONTAG

You don't get to choose how you're going to die, or when. You can only decide how you're going to live. Now!

JOAN BAEZ

I don't want to get to the end of my life and find that I just lived the length of it. I want to have lived the width of it as well.

DIANE ACKERMAN

If I had my life over again I should form the habit of nightly composing myself to thoughts of death. I would practice, as it were, the remembrance of death. There is no other practice which so intensifies life. Death, when it approaches, ought not to take one by surprise. It should be part of the full expectancy of life. Without an ever-present sense of death life is insipid. You might as well live on the whites of eggs.

MURIEL SPARK

Divorce

Changing husbands is only changing troubles.

KATHLEEN NORRIS

In our family we don't divorce men—we bury them.

RUTH GORDON

If divorce has increased one thousand percent, don't blame the women's movement. Blame our obsolete sex roles on which our marriages are based.

BETTY FRIEDAN

Marriages don't last. When I meet a guy, the first question I ask myself is: Is this the man I want my children to spend their weekends with?

RITA RUDNER

The courts cannot garnish a father's salary, nor freeze his account, nor seize his property on behalf of his children, in our society. Apparently this is because a kid is not a car or a couch or a boat.

JUNE JORDAN

A divorce is like an amputation: you survive it, but there's less of you.

MARGARET ATWOOD

Being divorced is like being hit by a Mack truck. If you live through it, you start looking very carefully to the right and to the left.

JEAN KERR

Divorced men are more likely to meet their car payments than their child support obligations.

SUSAN FALUDI

If you made a list of reasons why any couple got married, and another list of the reasons for their divorce, you'd have a hell of a lot of overlapping.

MIGNON MCLAUGHLIN

The desire to get married, which—I regret to say, I believe is basic and primal in women—is followed almost immediately by an equally basic and primal urge—which is to be single again.

NORA EPHRON

Doctors

One should only see a psychiatrist out of boredom.

MURIEL SPARK

I always say shopping is cheaper than a psychiatrist.

TAMMY FAYE BAKKER

Analysts keep having to pick away at the scab that the patient tries to form between himself and the analyst to cover his wounds. [The analyst] keeps the surface raw, so that the wound will heal properly.

JANET MALCOLM

Never go to a doctor whose office plants have died.

ERMA BOMBECK

[My whole life was] devoted unreservedly to the service of my sex. The study and practice of medicine is, in my thought, but one means to a great end, for which my very soul yearns with intensest emotion. . . . The true ennoblement of woman, the full harmonious development of her unknown nature, and the consequent redemption of the whole human race.

DR. ELIZABETH BLACKWELL

Doctors always think anybody doing something they aren't is a quack; also they think all patients are idiots.

FLANNERY O'CONNOR

The doctor's motto: Have patients.

ETHEL WATTS MUMFORD

Heart surgeons do not have the world's smallest egos: when you ask them to name the world's three leading practitioners, they never can remember the names of the other two.

SARA PARETSKY

I had never gone to a doctor in my adult life, feeling instinctively that doctors meant either cutting or, just as bad, diet.

CARSON MCCULLERS

Domestic Life

The fantasy of every Australian man is to have two women— one cleaning and the other dusting.

MAUREEN MURPHY

By and large, mothers and housewives are the only workers who do not have regular time off. They are the great vacationless class.

ANNE MORROW LINDBERGH

The labor of keeping house is labor in its most naked state, for labor is toil that never finishes, toil that has to begin again the moment it is completed, toil that is destroyed and consumed by the life process.

MARY MCCARTHY

I believe that all women, but especially housewives, tend to think in lists. . . . The idea of a series of items, following one another docilely, forms the only possible reasonable approach to life if you have to live it with a home and a husband and children, none of whom would dream of following one another docilely.

SHIRLEY JACKSON

Cleaning your house while your kids are still growing up is like shoveling the walk before it stops snowing.

PHYLLIS DILLER

I have too many fantasies to be a housewife. I guess I *am* a fantasy.

MARILYN MONROE

Like plowing, housework makes the ground ready for the germination of family life. The kids will not invite a teacher home if beer cans litter the living room. The family isn't likely to have breakfast together if somebody didn't remember to buy eggs, milk, or muffins. Housework maintains an orderly setting in which family life can flourish.

LETTY COTTIN POGREBIN

A man's home may seem to be his castle on the outside; inside it is more often his nursery.

CLARE BOOTHE LUCE

I don't like the terms "housewife" and "homemaker." I prefer to be called "Domestic Goddess" . . . it's more descriptive.

ROSEANNE

Woman's work! Housework's the hardest work in the world. That's why men won't do it.

EDNA FERBER

The fact is that men still do rather consistently undervalue or devalue women's powers as serious contributors to civilization except as homemakers.

MAY SARTON

The labor of women in the house, certainly, enables men to produce more wealth than they otherwise could; and in this way women are economic factors in society. But so are horses.

CHARLOTTE PERKINS GILMAN

Dreams

The future belongs to those who believe in the beauty of their dreams.

ELEANOR ROOSEVELT

The armored cars of dreams, contrived to let us do so many a dangerous thing.

ELIZABETH BISHOP

What else are we gonna live by if not dreams? We need to believe in something. What would really drive us crazy is to believe this reality we run into every day is all there is. If I don't believe that there's a happy ending out there—that will-you-marry-me in the sky—I can't keep working today.

JILL ROBINSON

I believe that dreams transport us through the underside of our days, and that if we wish to become acquainted with the dark side of what we are, the signposts are there, waiting for us to translate them.

GAIL GODWIN

It is in our idleness, in our dreams, that the submerged truth sometimes comes to the top.

VIRGINIA WOOLF

Dreams are great. When they disappear you may still be here, but you will have ceased to live.

LADY NANCY ASTOR

Dreams are . . . illustrations from the book your soul is writing about you.

MARSHA NORMAN

My dreams have become puny with the reality my life has become.

IMELDA MARCOS

Women have to summon up courage to fulfill dormant dreams.

ALICE WALKER

There are people who put their dreams in a little box and say, "Yes, I've got dreams, of course, I've got dreams." Then they put the box away and bring it out once in a while to look in it, and yep, they're still there. These are *great* dreams, but they never even get out of the box. It takes an uncommon amount of guts to put your dreams on the line, to hold them up and say, "How good or how bad am I?" That's where courage comes in.

ERMA BOMBECK

Drugs

All dope can do for you is kill you . . . the long hard way. And it can kill the people you love right along with you.

BILLIE HOLIDAY

Having a wonderful time. Wish I were here.

CARRIE FISHER

There seems to be no stopping drug frenzy once it takes hold of a nation. What starts with an innocuous HUGS, NOT DRUGS bumper sticker soon leads to wild talk of shooting dealers and making urine tests a condition for employment—anywhere.

BARBARA EHRENREICH

Reality is just a crutch for people who can't cope with drugs.

LILY TOMLIN

Cocaine habit-forming? Of course not. I ought to know. I've been using it for years.

TALLULAH BANKHEAD

The only merciful thing about drug abuse is the speed with which it devastates you. Alcoholics can take decades to destroy themselves and everyone they touch. The drug addict can accomplish this in a year or two. Of course, suicide is even more efficient.

RITA MAE BROWN

If you think dope is for kicks and for thrills, you're out of your mind. There are more kicks to be had in a good case of paralytic polio or by living in an iron lung. If you think you need stuff to play music or sing, you're crazy. It can fix you so you can't play nothing or sing nothing.

BILLIE HOLIDAY

Education

Good teaching is one-fourth preparation and three-fourths theater.

GAIL GODWIN

Children require guidance and sympathy far more than instruction.

ANNIE SULLIVAN

I read Shakespeare and the Bible, and I can shoot dice. That's what I call a liberal education.

TALLULAH BANKHEAD

I do not believe in a child world. It is a fantasy world. I believe the child should be taught from the very first that the whole world is his world, that adult and child share one world, that all generations are needed.

PEARL S. BUCK

The system—the American one, at least—is a vast and noble experiment. It has been polestar and exemplar for other nations. But from kindergarten until she graduates from college the girl is treated in it exactly like her brothers. She studies the same subjects, becomes proficient at the same sports. Oh, it is a magnificent lore she learns, education for the mind beyond anything Jane Austen or Saint Theresa or even Mrs. Pankhurst ever dreamed. It is truly Utopian. But Utopia was never meant to exist on this disheveled planet.

PHYLLIS MCGINLEY

One thing that never ceases to amaze me, along with the growth of vegetation from the earth and of hair from the head, is the growth of understanding.

ALICE WALKER

The academy is not paradise. But learning is a place where paradise can be created.

BELL HOOKS

In real life, I assure you, there is no such thing as algebra.

FRAN LEBOWITZ

If education is always to be conceived along the same antiquated lines of a mere transmission of knowledge, there is little to be hoped from it in the bettering of man's future. For what is the use transmitting knowledge if the individual's total development lags behind?

MARIA MONTESSORI

Any teacher can take a child to the classroom, but not every teacher can make him learn. He will not work joyously unless he feels that liberty is his, whether he is busy or at rest; he must feel the flush of victory and the heart-sinking of disappointment before he takes with a will the tasks distasteful to him and resolves to dance his way bravely through a dull routine of textbooks.

HELEN KELLER

That is what learning is. You suddenly understand something you've understood all your life, but in a new way.

DORIS LESSING

Empowerment

We fought hard. We gave it our best. We did what was right and we made a difference.

GERALDINE A. FERRARO

I don't want to be a passenger in my own life.

DIANE ACKERMAN

Power is the ability to do good things for others.

BROOKE ASTOR

The thing women have got to learn is that nobody gives you power. You just take it.

ROSEANNE

I think that education is power. I think that being able to communicate with people is power. One of my main goals on the planet is to encourage people to empower themselves.

OPRAH WINFREY

But I have noticed this about ambitious men, or men in power—they fear even the slightest and least likely threat to it.

MARY STEWART

We should try to bring to any power what we have as women. We will destroy it all if we try to imitate that absolutely unfeeling, driving ambition that we have seen coming at us across the desk.

COLLEEN DEWHURST

We have learned that power is a positive force if it is used for positive purposes.

ELIZABETH DOLE

Once, power was considered a masculine attribute. In fact, power has no sex.

KATHARINE GRAHAM

If you're talking about people without power, then essentially the only power you have is your combined energy, your combined visibility.

ANGELA DAVIS

I am a woman in the prime of life, with certain powers and those powers severely limited by authorities whose faces I rarely see.

ADRIENNE RICH

Environment

We won't have a society if we destroy the environment.

MARGARET MEAD

Like the resource it seeks to protect, wildlife conservation must be dynamic, changing as conditions change, seeking always to become more effective.

RACHEL CARSON

To me the outdoors is what you must pass through in order to get from your apartment into a taxicab.

FRAN LEBOWITZ

The best remedy for those who are afraid, lonely, or unhappy is to go outside, somewhere where they can be quite alone with the heavens, nature, and God. Because only then does one feel that all is as it should be and that God wishes to see people happy amidst the simple beauty of nature.

ANNE FRANK

The maltreatment of the natural world and its impoverishment leads to the impoverishment of the human soul. It is related to the outburst of violence in human society. To save the natural world today means to save what is human in humanity.

RAISA M. GORBACHEV

In terms of the biology of the planet, *development* is a euphemism for *destruction*.

HELEN CALDICOTT

Feeling that morality has nothing to do with the way you use the resources of the world is an idea that can't persist much longer. If it does, then we won't.

BARBARA KINGSOLVER

I had assumed that the Earth, the spirit of the Earth, noticed exceptions—those who wantonly damage it and those who do not. But the Earth is wise. It has given itself into the keeping of all, and all are therefore accountable.

ALICE WALKER

Entire species of animals have been exterminated, or reduced to so small a remnant that their survival is doubtful. Forests have been despoiled by uncontrolled and excessive cutting of lumber; grasslands have been destroyed by overgrazing . . . We have much to accomplish before we can feel assured of passing on to future generations a land as richly endowed in natural wealth as the one we live in.

RACHEL CARSON

Ethics

We pay a price when we deprive children of the exposure to the values, principles and education they need to make them good citizens.

SANDRA DAY O'CONNOR

I cannot and will not cut my conscience to fit this year's fashions.

LILLIAN HELLMAN

The act of acting morally is behaving *as if everything we do matters.*

GLORIA STEINEM

It is no wonder we behave badly, we are literally ignorant of the laws of ethics, which is the simplest of sciences, the most necessary, the most continuously needed. The childish misconduct of our "revolted youth" is quite equaled by that of older people, and neither young nor old seem to have any understanding of the reasons why conduct is "good" or "bad."

CHARLOTTE PERKINS GILMAN

The Department of Justice is committed to asking one central question of everything we do: What is the right thing to do? Now that can produce debate, and I want it to be spirited debate. I want the lawyers of America to be able to call me and tell me: Janet, have you lost your mind?

JANET WOOD RENO

Unfortunately, moral beauty in art—like physical beauty in a person—is extremely perishable. It is nowhere so durable as artistic or intellectual beauty. Moral beauty has a tendency to decay very rapidly into sententiousness or untimeliness.

SUSAN SONTAG

Since when do grown men and women, who presume to hold high government office and exercise what they think of as "moral leadership," require ethics officers to tell them whether it is or isn't permissible to grab the secretary's behind or redirect public funds to their own personal advantage?

MEG GREENFIELD

While it is generally agreed that the visible expressions and agencies are necessary instruments, civilization seems to depend far more fundamentally upon the moral and intellectual qualities of human beings—upon the spirit that animates mankind.

MARY BEARD

It is far easier for a woman to lead a blameless life than it is for a man; all she has to do is to avoid sexual intercourse like the plague.

ANGELA CARTER

Exercise

The only reason I would take up jogging is so that I could hear heavy breathing again.

ERMA BOMBECK

My grandmother started walking five miles a day when she was sixty—she's ninety-seven today and we don't know where the hell she is.

ELLEN DEGENERES

Contrary to popular cable TV-induced opinion, aerobics have absolutely nothing to do with squeezing our body into hideous shiny Spandex, grinning like a deranged orangutan, and doing cretinous dance steps to debauched disco music.

CYNTHIA HEIMEL

I think anyone who comes upon a Nautilus machine suddenly will agree with me that its prototype was clearly invented at some time in history when torture was considered a reasonable alternative to diplomacy.

ANNA QUINDLEN

Sedentary people are apt to have sluggish minds. A sluggish mind is apt to be reflected in flabbiness of body and in a dullness of expression that invites no interest and gets none.

ROSE FITZGERALD KENNEDY

As long as my body is in shape, my mind is working at its full capacity.

VICTORIA PRINCIPAL

To me, good health is more than just exercise and diet. It's really a point of view and a mental attitude you have about yourself.

ANGELA LANSBURY

Experience

If we could sell our experiences for what they cost us, we'd all be millionaires.

ABIGAIL VAN BUREN

And I think that's important, to know how the water's gone over the dam before you start to describe it. It helps to have been over the dam yourself.

E. ANNIE PROULX

Doesn't all experience crumble in the end to mere literary material?

ELLEN GLASGOW

A woman's life can really be a succession of lives, each revolving around some emotionally compelling situation or challenge, and each marked off by some intense experience.

WALLIS SIMPSON,
DUCHESS OF WINDSOR

The basic experience of everyone is the experience of human limitation.

FLANNERY O'CONNOR

I'd do these disappearing acts. I'd pass through some seedy town with a pinball arcade, fall in with people who worked on the machines, people staying alive shoplifting, whatever. They don't know who you are: "Why are you driving that white Mercedes? Oh, you're driving it for somebody else." You know, make up some name and hang out. Great experiences, almost like *The Prince and the Pauper*.

JONI MITCHELL

In my experience, there is only one motivation, and that is desire. No reasons or principles contain it or stand against it.

JANE SMILEY

[Experience is] how life catches up with us and teaches us to love and forgive each other.

JUDY COLLINS

The notion of a universality of human experience is a confidence trick and the notion of a universality of female experience is a clever confidence trick.

ANGELA CARTER

I long to put the experience of fifty years at once into your young lives, to give you at once the key to that treasure chamber every gem of which has cost me tears and struggles and prayers, but you must work for these inward treasures yourselves.

HARRIET BEECHER STOWE

I have always grown from my problems and challenges, from the things that don't work out, that's when I've really learned.

CAROL BURNETT

The events in our lives happen in a sequence in time, but in their significance to ourselves, they find their own order . . . the continuous thread of revelation.

EUDORA WELTY

Failure

Flops are a part of life's menu and I've never been a girl to miss out on any of the courses.

ROSALIND RUSSELL

The only difference between a rut and a grave is their dimensions.

ELLEN GLASGOW

It is better to be young in your failures than old in your successes.

FLANNERY O'CONNOR

You may be disappointed if you fail, but you are doomed if you don't try.

BEVERLY SILLS

Supposing you have tried and failed again and again. You may have a fresh start any moment you choose, for this thing that we call "failure" is not the falling down, but the staying down.

MARY PICKFORD

You must accept that you might fail; then, if you do your best and still don't win, at least you can be satisfied that you've tried. If you don't accept failure as a possibility, you don't set high goals, you don't branch out, you don't try—you don't take the risk.

ROSALYNN CARTER

I don't believe in failure. It is not failure if you enjoyed the process.

OPRAH WINFREY

I wasn't afraid to fail. Something good always comes out of failure.

ANNE BAXTER

Faith

Conversion for me was not a Damascus Road experience. I slowly moved into an intellectual acceptance of what my intuition had always known.

MADELEINE L'ENGLE

Any God I ever felt in church I brought in with me.

ALICE WALKER

Not truth, but faith, it is that keeps the world alive.

EDNA ST. VINCENT MILLAY

While I know myself as a creation of God, I am also obligated to realize and remember that everyone else and everything else are also God's creation.

MAYA ANGELOU

I do not pray for success. I ask for faithfulness.

MOTHER TERESA

Faith is not belief. Belief is passive. Faith is active.
EDITH HAMILTON

There is a place where we are always alone with our own mortality, where we must simply have something greater than ourselves to hold onto—God or history or politics or literature or a belief in the healing power of love, or even righteous anger. . . . A reason to believe, a way to take the world by the throat and insist that there is more to this life than we have ever imagined.
DOROTHY ALLISON

Without faith, nothing is possible. With it, nothing is impossible.
MARY MCLEOD BETHUNE

My faith
is a great weight
hung on a small wire,
as doth the spider
hang her baby on a thin web.
ANNE SEXTON

Yes, I have doubted. I have wandered off the path, but I always return. It is intuitive, an intrinsic, built-in sense of direction. I seem always to find my way home. My faith has wavered but saved me.
HELEN HAYES

Fame

Until you've lost your reputation, you never realize what a burden it was or what freedom really is.

MARGARET MITCHELL

Fame lost its appeal for me when I went into a public restroom and an autograph seeker handed me a pen and paper under the stall door.

MARLO THOMAS

I can ruin my reputation in five minutes; I don't need help.

MARTHA GRAHAM

I don't care what is written about me so long as it isn't true.

DOROTHY PARKER

The fame you earn has a different taste from the fame that is forced upon you.

GLORIA VANDERBILT

In the final analysis, it's true that fame is unimportant. No matter how great a man is, the size of his funeral usually depends on the weather.

ROSEMARY CLOONEY

It is a mark of many famous people that they cannot part with their brightest hour.

LILLIAN HELLMAN

I don't mind if my skull ends up on a shelf as long as it's got my name on it.

DEBBIE HARRY

Fame will go by and, so long, I've had you, fame. If it goes by, I've always known it was fickle. So at least it's something I experience, but that's not where I live.

MARILYN MONROE

You wonder about people who made a fortune, and you always think they drank it up or stuck it up their nose. That's not usually what brings on the decline. It's usually the battle to keep your creative child alive while keeping your business shark alive. You have to develop cunning and shrewdness and other things which are well suited to the arts.

JONI MITCHELL

Family

The presidency is temporary—but the family is permanent.

YVONNE DE GAULLE,
WIFE OF THE FRENCH PRESIDENT

The striking point about our model family is not simply the compete-compete, consume-consume style of life it urges us to follow. . . . The striking point, in the face of all the propaganda, is how few Americans actually live this way.

LOUISE KAPP HOWE

In your standard-issue family—of which few remain, but on which our expectations are still based—there are parents and there are children. The way you know which are which, aside from certain size and age differences and despite any behavior similarities, is that the parents are the bossy ones.

DELIA EPHRON

I know why families were created, with all their imperfections. They humanize you. They are made to make you forget yourself occasionally, so that the beautiful balance of life is not destroyed.

ANAÏS NIN

Having family responsibilities and concerns just has to make you a more understanding person.

SANDRA DAY O'CONNOR

You hear a lot of dialogue on the death of the American family. Families aren't dying. They're merging into big conglomerates.

ERMA BOMBECK

As to the family, I have never understood how that fits in with the other ideals—or, indeed, why it should be an ideal at all. A group of closely related persons living under one roof; it is a convenience, often a necessity, sometimes a pleasure, sometimes the reverse; but who first exalted it as admirable, an almost religious ideal?

ROSE MACAULAY

It's only when you grow up, and step back from [your father], or leave him for your own career and your own home—it's only then that you can measure his greatness and fully appreciate it. Pride reinforces love.

MARGARET TRUMAN

Families are nothing more than the idolatry of duty.

ANN OAKLEY

I don't believe that the accident of birth makes people sisters or brothers. It makes them siblings. Gives them mutuality of parentage. Sisterhood and brotherhood is a condition people have to work at.

MAYA ANGELOU

The family is the building block for whatever solidarity there is in society.

JILL RUCKELSHAUS

Our generation's social revolution taught us that family life needs protection. Our laws, policies, and society as a whole must support families.

MARILYN QUAYLE

The tie is stronger than that between father and son and father and daughter. . . . The bond is also more complex than the one between mother and daughter. For a woman, a son offers the best chance to know the mysterious male existence.

CAROLE KLEIN

The family is the basic cell of government: it is where we are trained to believe that we are human beings or that we are chattel, it is where we are trained to see the sex and race divisions and become callous to injustice even if it is done to ourselves, to accept as biological a full system of authoritarian government.

GLORIA STEINEM

Fatherhood

A man prides himself on his strength—but when his child is born discovers overnight that strength is not enough, and that he must learn gentleness.

PAM BROWN

A dad is a man haunted by death, fears, anxieties. But who seems to his children the haven from all harm. And who makes them certain that whatever happens—it will all come right.

CLARA ORTEGA

How sad that men would base an entire civilization on the principle of paternity, upon the legal ownership and presumed responsibility for children, and then never get to know their sons and daughters very well.

PHYLLIS CHESLER

We criticize mothers for closeness. We criticize fathers for distance. How many of us have expected less from our fathers and appreciated what they gave us more? How many of us always let them off the hook?

ELLEN GOODMAN

The human father has to be confronted and recognized as human, as man who created a child and then, by his absence, left the child fatherless and then Godless.

ANAÏS NIN

Like all children I had taken my father for granted. Now that I had lost him, I felt an emptiness that could never be filled.

But I did not let myself cry, believing as a Muslim that tears pull a spirit earthward and won't let it be free.

BENAZIR BHUTTO

Safe, for a child, is his father's hand, holding him tight.

MARION C. GARRETTY

Fear

Nothing in life is to be feared. It is only to be understood.

MARIE CURIE

The key to change . . . is to let go of fear.

ROSANNE CASH

We're frightened of what makes us different.

ANNE RICE

By the time we are women, fear is as familiar to us as air. It is our element. We live in it, we inhale it, we exhale it, and most of the time we do not even notice it. Instead of "I am afraid," we say, "I don't want to," or "I don't know how," or "I can't."

ANDREA DWORKIN

I have a lot of things to prove to myself. One is that I can live my life fearlessly.

OPRAH WINFREY

Anything scares me, anything scares anyone but really after all considering how dangerous everything is nothing is really very frightening.

GERTRUDE STEIN

I have not ceased being fearful, but I have ceased to let fear control me. I have accepted fear as a part of life—specifically the fear of change, the fear of the unknown; and I have gone ahead despite the pounding in my heart that says: Turn back, turn back, you'll die if you venture too far.

ERICA JONG

If you banish fear, nothing terribly bad can happen to you.

MARGARET BOURKE-WHITE

Never, never let a person know you're frightened.

MAYA ANGELOU

Feminism

I became a feminist as an alternative to becoming a masochist.

SALLY KEMPTON

The major concrete achievement of the women's movement in the 1970s was the Dutch treat.

NORA EPHRON

During the feminist revolution, the battle lines were again simple. It was easy to tell the enemy, he was the one with the penis. This is no longer strictly true. Some men are okay now. We're allowed to like them again. We still have to keep them in line, of course, but we no longer have to shoot them on sight.

CYNTHIA HEIMEL

A liberated woman is one who has sex before marriage and a job after.

GLORIA STEINEM

No one can argue any longer about the rights of women. It's like arguing about earthquakes.

LILLIAN HELLMAN

The sadness of the women's movement is that they don't allow the necessity of love. See, I don't personally trust any revolution where love is not allowed.

MAYA ANGELOU

People call me a feminist whenever I express sentiments that differentiate me from a doormat or a prostitute.

REBECCA WEST

I would even go to Washington . . . just to glimpse Jane Q. Public being sworn as the first female president of the United States, while her husband holds the Bible and wears a silly pillbox hat and matching coat.

ANNA QUINDLEN

One of the things about equality is not just that you be treated equally to a man, but that you treat yourself equally to the way you treat a man.

MARLO THOMAS

Toughness doesn't have to come in a pinstripe suit.

DIANNE FEINSTEIN

Our struggle today is not to have a female Einstein get appointed as an assistant professor. It is for a woman schlemiel to get as quickly promoted as a male schlemiel.

BELLA ABZUG

I have a brain and a uterus, and I use both.

PATRICIA SCHROEDER

A young man put the old question, "Do you really care about this equal rights business? Wouldn't you rather be adored?" My answer was firm. "No, I would rather *not* be adored. It's been tried, but it just makes me nervous."

CAROLINE BIRD

People have been writing premature obituaries on the women's movement since its beginning.

ELLEN GOODMAN

I never understood women's liberation. I always got what I wanted from men without asking.

MARTHA GRAHAM

Women are not men's equals in anything except responsibility. We are not their inferiors, either, or even their superiors. We are, quite simply, different races.

PHYLLIS MCGINLEY

It occurred to me when I was thirteen and wearing white gloves and Mary Janes and going to dancing school, that no one should have to dance backward all their lives.

JILL RUCKELSHAUS

Women want a family life that glitters and is stable. They don't want some lump spouse watching ice hockey in the late hours of his eighteenth beer. They want a family that is so much fun and is so smart that they look forward to Thanksgiving rather than regarding it with a shudder. That's the glitter part. The stable part is, obviously, they don't want to be one bead on a long necklace of wives. They want, just like men, fun, love, fame, money, and power. And equal pay for equal work.

CAROLYN SEE

[Women want] the seemingly impossible: that men treat them with the respect and fairmindedness with which they treat most men.

JOYCE CAROL OATES

I'm furious about the Women's Liberationists. They keep getting up on soapboxes and proclaiming that women are brighter than men. That's true, but it should be kept very quiet or it ruins the whole racket.

ANITA LOOS

The most exciting thing about women's liberation is that this century will be able to take advantage of talent and potential genius that have been wasted because of taboos.

HELEN REDDY

We've chosen the path to equality; don't let them turn us around.

GERALDINE A. FERRARO

Women's liberation is just a lot of foolishness. It's the men who are discriminated against. They can't bear children. And no one's likely to do anything about that.

GOLDA MEIR

As long as the feminine mystique masks the emptiness of the housewife's role...there will never be enough Prince Charmings, or enough therapists to break that pattern.

BETTY FRIEDAN

In the new code of laws which I suppose will be necessary for you to make, I desire you would remember the ladies and be more generous and favorable to them than your ancestors. Do not put such unlimited power into the hands of husbands. Remember, all men would be tyrants if they could. If particular care and attention is not paid to the ladies, we are determined to forment a rebellion, and will not hold ourselves bound by any laws in which we have no voice or representation.

ABIGAIL ADAMS

Film

Does art reflect life? In movies, yes. Because more than any other art form, films have been a mirror held up to society's porous face.

MARJORIE ROSEN

The immense popularity of American movies abroad demonstrates that Europe is the unfinished negative of which America is the proof.

MARY MCCARTHY

Hollywood—an emotional Detroit.

LILLIAN GISH

The words "Kiss Kiss Bang Bang" which I saw on an Italian movie poster, are perhaps the briefest statement imaginable of the basic appeal of movies.

PAULINE KAEL

It struck me that the movies had spent more than half a century saying "They lived happily ever after" and the following quarter-century warning that they'll be lucky to make it through the weekend. Possibly now we are entering a third era in which the movies will be sounding a note of cautious optimism: You know it just might work.

NORA EPHRON

The movies are still where it happens, not for much longer perhaps, but the movies are still the art form that uses the material of our lives and the art form that we use.

PAULINE KAEL

Food/Dieting

Beauty is in the eyes and mind of the eater. Even if the salmon has been dropped on the linoleum, it comes up smiling. Let the guests remain in equally smiling ignorance.

MADELEINE BINGHAM

It's an interesting fact that babies who won't smile for love or money will smile for a vegetable. And the messier the vegetable the more they will smile.

JEAN KERR

What I love about cooking is that after a hard day, there is something comforting about the fact that if you melt butter and add flour and then hot stock, IT WILL GET THICK! It's a sure thing! It's a sure thing in the world where nothing is sure.

NORA EPHRON

Where do you go to get anorexia?

SHELLEY WINTERS

A food is not necessarily essential just because your child hates it.

KATHERINE WHITEHORN

I've been on a constant diet for the last two decades. I've lost a total of 789 pounds. By all accounts, I should be hanging from a charm bracelet.

ERMA BOMBECK

Cooking, like unrequited love, is all in the mind. Once a girl has decided her ex-boyfriend is a fat slob, she can forget all about him. . . . It is just the same with burned cakes.

MADELEINE BINGHAM

Cooked carrots: On way to mouth, drop in lap. Smuggle to garbage in napkin.

DELIA EPHRON

Upscale people are fixated with food simply because they are now able to eat so much of it without getting fat, and the reason they don't get fat is that they maintain a profligate level of calorie expenditure. The very same people whose evenings begin with melted goats cheese . . . get up at dawn to run, break for a mid-morning aerobics class, and watch the evening news while racing on a stationary bicycle.

BARBARA EHRENREICH

The way to a man's heart is through his stomach.

FANNY FERN

Whenever you see food beautifully arranged on a plate, you know someone's fingers have been all over it.

JULIA CHILD

Food is an important part of a balanced diet.

FRAN LEBOWITZ

She's so fat she's my two best friends. She wears stretch caftans. She's got more chins than the Chinese telephone directory.

JOAN RIVERS

Cooking is like love. It should be entered into with abandon or not at all.

HARRIET VAN HORNE

Nobody can cook as well as mother.

MARIA FLORIS

All real men love to eat.

MARLENE DIETRICH

Life itself is the proper binge.

JULIA CHILD

From the day on which she weighs 140, the chief excitement of a woman's life consists in spotting women who are fatter than she is.

HELEN ROWLAND

Freedom/Equality

No man may make another free.

ZORA NEALE HURSTON

In a society where the rights and potential of women are constrained, no man can be truly free. He may have power, but he will not have freedom.

MARY ROBINSON

The freer that women become, the freer men will be. Because when you enslave someone, you are enslaved.

LOUISE NEVELSON

The true exercise of freedom is—cannily and wisely and with grace—to move inside what space confines—and not seek to know what lies beyond and cannot be touched or tasted.

A. S. BYATT

Now men and women are separate and unequal. We should be hand in hand; in fact, we should have our arms around each other.

CLORIS LEACHMAN

But the whole point of liberation is that you get out. Restructure your life. Act by yourself.

JANE FONDA

Freedom makes a huge requirement of every human being. With freedom comes responsibility. For the person who is unwilling to grow up, the person who does not want to carry his own weight, this is a frightening prospect.

ELEANOR ROOSEVELT

We know the road to freedom has always been stalked by death.

ANGELA DAVIS

One distressing thing is the way men react to women who assert their equality: their ultimate weapon is to call them unfeminine. They think she is anti-male; they even whisper that she's probably a lesbian.

SHIRLEY CHISHOLM

Whatever my individual desires were to be free, I was not alone. There were many others who felt the same way.

ROSA PARKS

The oppressed never free themselves—they do not have the necessary strengths.

CLARE BOOTHE LUCE

It should be remarked that, as the principle of liberty is better understood, and more nobly interpreted, a broader protest is made in behalf of women. As men become aware that few have had a fair chance, they are inclined to say that no women have had a fair chance.

MARGARET FULLER

You know I work for the liberation of all people, because when I liberate myself, I'm liberating other people.

FANNIE LOU HAMER

I had reasoned this out in my mind, there were two things I had a right to: liberty and death. If I could not have one, I would have the other, for no man should take me alive.

HARRIET TUBMAN

A liberated woman is one who feels confident in herself, and is happy in what she is doing. She is a person who has a sense of self. . . . It all comes down to freedom of choice.

BETTY FORD

I have crossed over on the backs of Sojourner Truth, Harriet Tubman, Fannie Lou Hamer, and Madam C. J. Walker. Because of them I can now live the dream. I am the seed of the free, and I know it. I intend to bear great fruit.

OPRAH WINFREY

Many whites, even white Southerners, told me that even though it may have seemed like the blacks were being freed, they felt more free and at ease themselves.

ROSA PARKS

Friendship

Accountability in friendship is the equivalent of love without strategy.

ANITA BROOKNER

True friends are those who really know you but love you anyway.

EDNA BUCHANAN

I suppose there is one friend in the life of each of us who seems not a separate person, however dear and beloved, but an expansion, an interpretation, of one's self, the very meaning of one's soul.

EDITH WHARTON

They *are* love, those rare, binding early friendships. Not everyone has them, and almost no one gets more than one. The others, the later ones, are not the same. These grow in a soil found only in the country of the young, and are possible only there, because their medium is unbroken time and proximity and discovery, and later there is not enough of any of those for the total, ongoing immersions that these friendships are.

ANNE RIVERS SIDDONS

Wit . . . is, after all, a form of arousal. We challenge one another to be funnier and smarter. It's high-energy play. It's the way friends make love to one another.

ANNE GOTTLIEB

Only solitary men know the full joys of friendship. Others have their family, but to a solitary and an exile his friends are everything.

WILLA CATHER

I have lost friends, some by death . . . others by sheer inability to cross the street.

VIRGINIA WOOLF

It is prudent to pour the oil of delicate politeness upon the machinery of friendship.

COLETTE

God gives us our relatives; thank God we can choose our friends.

ETHEL WATTS MUMFORD

The growth of true friendship may be a lifelong affair.

SARAH ORNE JEWETT

I can trust my friends. . . . These people force me to examine myself, encourage me to grow.

CHER

Lots of people want to ride with you in the limo, but what you want is someone who will take the bus with you when the limo breaks down.

OPRAH WINFREY

When someone tells you the truth, lets you think for yourself, experience your own emotions, he is treating you as a true equal. As a friend.

WHITNEY OTTO

I have learned that to have a good friend is the purest of all God's gifts, for it is a love that has no exchange of payment.

FRANCES FARMER

It's the friends you can call up at 4 a.m. that matter.

MARLENE DIETRICH

The truth is, friendship is to me every bit as sacred and eternal as marriage.

KATHERINE MANSFIELD

Gender Gap

I do not believe in sex distinction in literature, law, politics, or trade—or that modesty and virtue are more becoming to women than to men, but wish we had more of it everywhere.

BELVA LOCKWOOD

Show me a woman who doesn't feel guilty and I'll show you a man.

ERICA JONG

It would be a futile attempt to fit women into a masculine pattern of attitudes, skills and abilities and disastrous to force them to suppress their specifically female characteristics and abilities by keeping up the pretense that there are no differences between the sexes.

ARIANNA HUFFINGTON

In the theory of gender I began from zero. There is no masculine power or privilege I did not covet. But slowly, step by step, decade by decade, I was forced to acknowledge that even a woman of abnormal will cannot escape her hormonal identity.

CAMILLE PAGLIA

To me gender is not physical at all, but is altogether insubstantial. It is soul, perhaps, it is talent, it is taste, it is environment, it is how one feels, it is light and shade, it is inner music . . . It is the essentialness of oneself.

JAN MORRIS

The mind is not sex-typed.

MARGARET MEAD

Government

Democracy cannot be static. Whatever is static is dead.

ELEANOR ROOSEVELT

How could I possibly overthrow the government when I can't even keep my dog down?

DOROTHY PARKER

Women are being considered as candidates for Vice President of the United States because it is the worst job in America. It's amazing that men will take it. A job with real power is First Lady. I'd be willing to run for that. As far as the men who are running for President are concerned, they aren't even people I would date.

NORA EPHRON

I don't mind how much my ministers talk—as long as they do what I say.

MARGARET THATCHER

The stakes . . . are too high for government to be a spectator sport.

BARBARA JORDAN

If you join government, calmly make your contribution and move on. Don't go along to get along; do your best and when you have to—and you will—leave, and be something else.

PEGGY NOONAN

They say women talk too much. If you have worked in Congress you know that the filibuster was invented by men.

CLARE BOOTHE LUCE

Washington, is, for one thing, the news capital of the world. And for another, it is a company town. Most of the interesting people in Washington either work for the government or write about it.

SALLY QUINN

If we get a government that reflects more of what this country is really about, we can turn the country—and the economy—around.

BELLA ABZUG

What you have when everyone wears the same playclothes for all occasions, is addressed by nickname, expected to participate in Show and Tell, and bullied out of any desire for privacy, is not democracy; it is kindergarten.

MISS MANNERS (JUDITH MARTIN)

We're half the people; we should be half the Congress.

JEANNETTE RANKIN

Growing Up

You grow up the day you have your first real laugh—at yourself.

ETHEL BARRYMORE

Maturity: A stoic response to endless reality.

CARRIE FISHER

You have a wonderful child. Then, when he's thirteen, gremlins carry him away and leave in his place a stranger who gives you not a moment's peace.

JILL EIKENBERRY

Remember that as a teenager you are at the last stage in your life when you will be happy to hear that the phone is for you.

FRAN LEBOWITZ

I didn't belong as a kid, and that always bothered me. If only I'd known that one day my differentness would be an asset, then my early life would have been much easier.

BETTE MIDLER

There comes a time when you have to face the fact that Dad has forgotten how to do algebra.

CHARLOTTE GRAY

Every human being on this earth is born with a tragedy that he has to grow up. That he has to leave the nest, the security, and go out to do battle. He has to lose everything that is lovely and fight for a new loveliness of his own making, and it's a tragedy. A lot of people don't have the courage to do it.

HELEN HAYES

When I was growing up I always wanted to be someone. Now I realize I should have been more specific.

LILY TOMLIN

Adolescence is like cactus.

ANAÏS NIN

Adolescence is a twentieth-century invention most parents approach with dread and look back on with the relief of survivors.

FAYE MOSKOWITZ

Growing up female in America. What a liability! You grew up with your ears full of cosmetic ads, love songs, advice columns, whoreoscopes, Hollywood gossip, and moral dilemmas on the level of tv soap operas. What litanies the advertisers of the good life chanted at you! What curious catechisms!

ERICA JONG

Happiness

When one door of happiness closes, another opens; but often we look so long at the closed door that we do not see the one which has been opened for us.

HELEN KELLER

Someone once asked me what I regarded as the three most important requirements for happiness. My answer was: "A feeling that you have been honest with yourself and those around you; a feeling that you have done the best you could both in your personal life and in your work; and the ability to love others."

ELEANOR ROOSEVELT

Don't wish me happiness—I don't expect to be happy . . . it's gotten beyond that somehow. Wish me courage and strength and a sense of humor—I will need them all.

ANNE MORROW LINDBERGH

Happiness is good health and a bad memory.

INGRID BERGMAN

Happiness is a matter of one's most ordinary everyday mode of consciousness being busy and lively and unconcerned with self. To be damned is for one's ordinary everyday mode of consciousness to be unremitting agonizing preoccupation with self.

IRIS MURDOCH

There is no such thing as inner peace. There is only nervousness and death.

FRAN LEBOWITZ

If only we'd stop trying to be happy, we could have a pretty good time.

EDITH WHARTON

Heritage

We are linked by blood, and blood is memory without language.

JOYCE CAROL OATES

I have not much interest in anyone's personal history after the tenth year, not even my own. Whatever one was to be was all prepared before that.

KATHERINE ANNE PORTER

Guided by my heritage of a love of beauty and a respect for strength—in search of my mother's garden I found my own.

ALICE WALKER

One of the strengths I derive from my class background is that I am accustomed to contempt.

DOROTHY ALLISON

It is true that I was born in Iowa, but I can't speak for my twin sister.

ABIGAIL VAN BUREN (DEAR ABBY)

Human Nature

Superior people never make long visits.

MARIANNE MOORE

Everybody gets so much information all day long that they lose their common sense.

GERTRUDE STEIN

You take people as far as they will go, not as far as you would like them to go.

JEANNETTE RANKIN

It's the good girls who keep the diaries; the bad girls never have the time.

TALLULAH BANKHEAD

A closed mind is a dying mind.

EDNA FERBER

It is terribly amusing how many different climates of feeling one can go through in one day.

ANNE MORROW LINDBERGH

People who are always making allowances for themselves soon go bankrupt.

MARY PETTIBONE POOLE

People are prone to build a statue of the kind of person that it pleases them to be. And few people want to be forced to ask themselves, "What if there is no me like my statue?"

ZORA NEALE HURSTON

That's the truest sign of insanity—insane people are always sure they're just fine. It's only the sane people who are willing to admit they're crazy.

NORA EPHRON

I realized that if what we call human nature can be changed, then absolutely anything is possible. From that moment, my life changed.

SHIRLEY MACLAINE

Humor

Whatever you have read I have said is almost certainly untrue, except if it is funny, in which case I definitely said it.

TALLULAH BANKHEAD

He who laughs, lasts.

MARY PETTIBONE POOLE

Humor comes from self-confidence. There's an aggressive element to wit.

RITA MAE BROWN

If you could choose one characteristic that would get you through life, choose a sense of humor.

JENNIFER JONES

I think laughter may be a form of courage. . . . As humans we sometimes stand tall and look into the sun and laugh, and I think we are never more brave than when we do that.

LINDA ELLERBEE

If somebody makes me laugh, I'm his slave for life.

BETTE MIDLER

There's a hell of a difference between wisecracking and wit. Wit has truth to it; wisecracking is simply calisthenics with words.

DOROTHY PARKER

It's a difficult thing to like anybody else's ideas of being funny.

GERTRUDE STEIN

When humor goes, there goes civilization.

ERMA BOMBECK

He'd never laugh at my jokes. . . . I was a woman, meaning my relationship with humor should have been as an object, not a perpetrator.

ROSEANNE

Sexiness wears thin after a while and beauty fades, but to be married to a man who makes you laugh every day, ah, now that's a real treat!

JOANNE WOODWARD

Being a funny person does an awful lot of things to you. You feel that you mustn't get serious with people. They don't expect it from you, and they don't want to see it. You're not entitled to be serious, you're a clown, and they only want you to make them laugh.

FANNY BRICE

Hostility is expressed in a number of ways. One is laughter.

KATE MILLETT

Laughter is by definition healthy.

DORIS LESSING

A laugh is a terrible weapon.

KATE O'BRIEN

Ideas

No idea is so antiquated that it was not once modern. No idea is so modern that it will not someday be antiquated.

ELLEN GLASGOW

It's very good for an idea to be commonplace. The important thing is that a new idea should develop out of what is already there so that it soon becomes an old acquaintance. Old acquaintances aren't by any means always welcome, but at least one can't be mistaken as to who or what they are.

PENELOPE FITZGERALD

I learned to make my mind large, as the universe is large, so that there is room for paradoxes.

MAXINE HONG KINGSTON

Think wrongly, if you please, but in all cases think for yourself.

DORIS LESSING

There are no new ideas. There are only new ways of making them felt.

AUDRE LORDE

You can imprison a man, but not an idea. You can exile a man, but not an idea. You can kill a man, but not an idea.
BENAZIR BHUTTO

Thoughts are energy, and you can make your world or break your world by your thinking.
SUSAN L. TAYLOR

My ideas are a curse.
They spring from a radical discontent
With the awful order of things.
ANNE SEXTON

Illness

Illness is the night-side of life, a more onerous citizenship. Everyone who is born holds dual citizenship, in the kingdom of the well and in the kingdom of the sick. Although we all prefer to use only the good passport, sooner or later each of us is obliged, at least for a spell, to identify ourselves as citizens of that other place.
SUSAN SONTAG

I have never been anywhere but sick. In a sense sickness is a place, more instructive than a long trip to Europe, and it's always a place where there's no company, where nobody can follow. Sickness before death is a very appropriate thing and I think those who don't have it miss one of God's mercies.
FLANNERY O'CONNOR

Dearest Lord, may I see you today and every day in the person of your sick, and, whilst nursing them, minister unto you. Though you hide yourself behind the unattractive disguise of the irritable, the exacting, the unreasonable, may I still recognize you, and say: "Jesus, my patient, how sweet it is to serve you."

MOTHER TERESA

The sick soon come to understand that they live in a different world from that of the well and that the two cannot communicate.

JESSAMYN WEST

To you illness is negligible. You have learned that you can dominate yourself. You know that your body lags, but your soul proceeds upon its triumphant way.

ALICE FOOTE MACDOUGALL

Imagination

Imagination is the highest kite one can fly.

LAUREN BACALL

My imagination makes me human and makes me a fool; it gives me all the world and exiles me from it.

URSULA K. LE GUIN

Imagination, like memory, can transform lies to truths.
CRISTINA GARCIA

What man can imagine he may one day achieve.
NANCY HALE

Imagination makes cowards of us all.
ETHEL WATTS MUMFORD

Imagination and fiction make up more than three quarters of our real life.
SIMONE WEIL

The imagination needs moodling—long, inefficient, happy idling, dawdling, and puttering.
BRENDA UELAND

Write about winter in the summer. Describe Norway as Ibsen did, from a desk in Italy; describe Dublin as James Joyce did, from a desk in Paris. Willa Cather wrote her prairie novels in New York City; Mark Twain wrote *Huckleberry Finn* in Hartford, Connecticut. Recently, scholars learned that Walt Whitman rarely left his room.
ANNIE DILLARD

Jealousy

Jealousy, an uncontrollable passion. The Siamese twin of love.

MARLENE DIETRICH

Jealousy is all the fun you *think* they had.

ERICA JONG

Jealousy is the only evil we endure without becoming accustomed to it.

COLETTE

To jealousy, nothing is more frightful than laughter.

FRANÇOISE SAGAN

When people say: she's got everything, I've only one answer: I haven't had tomorrow.

ELIZABETH TAYLOR

Jealousy is the reverse of understanding, of sympathy, and of generous feeling. Never has jealousy added to character, never does it make the individual big and fine.

EMMA GOLDMAN

Jealousy in romance is like salt in food. A little can enhance the savor, but too much can spoil the pleasure and, under certain circumstances, can be life-threatening.

MAYA ANGELOU

Whoever had known sexual jealousy, that most destructive of emotions—and this would be so for men no less than women—had known madness and had now to know sympathy for someone who had been carried by jealousy this one terrible step too far, to murder.

DIANA TRILLING

Journalism

You should always believe all you read in newspapers, as this makes them more interesting.

ROSE MACAULAY

I see journalists as the manual workers, the laborers of the word. Journalism can only be literature when it is passionate.

MARGUERITE DURAS

Every journalist who is not too stupid or too full of himself to notice what is going on knows that what he does is morally indefensible. He is a kind of confidence man, preying on people's vanity, ignorance, or loneliness, gaining their trust and betraying them without remorse.

JANET MALCOLM

In journalism there has always been a tension between getting it first and getting it right.

ELLEN GOODMAN

Never joke with the press. Irony does not translate into newsprint.

ERICA JONG

To write weekly, to write daily, to write shortly, to write for busy people catching trains in the morning or for tired people coming home in the evening, is a heartbreaking task for men who know good writing from bad. They do it, but instinctively draw out of harm's way anything precious that might be damaged by contact with the public, or anything sharp that might irritate its skin.

VIRGINIA WOOLF

I was terrible at straight items. When I wrote obituaries, my mother said the only thing I ever got them to do was die in alphabetical order.

ERMA BOMBECK

When there is good news, and it is *news*, we do report it, but usually news is a record of human failure. Those wanting to celebrate human accomplishment are, as someone said, advised to go to the sports section.

LINDA ELLERBEE

Gossip is just news running ahead of itself in a red satin dress.

LIZ SMITH

Journalism—an ability to meet the challenge of filling space.

REBECCA WEST

Language

Male supremacy is fused into the language, so that every sentence both heralds and affirms it.

ANDREA DWORKIN

Language is political. That's why you and me, my brother and sister, that's why we sposed to choke our natural self into the weird, lying, barbarous, unreal, white speech and writing habits that the schools lay down like holy law. Because, in other words, the powerful don't play; they mean to keep that power, and those who are the powerless (you and me) better shape up—mimic/ape/suck—in the very image of the powerful, or the powerful will destroy you—you and your children.

JUNE JORDAN

Public speaking is done in the public tongue, the national or tribal language; and the language of our tribe is the men's language. Of course women learn it. We're not dumb. If you can tell Margaret Thatcher from Ronald Reagan, or Indira Gandhi from General Somoza, by anything they say, then tell me how. This is a man's world, so it talks a man's language.

URSULA K. LE GUIN

We might hypothetically possess ourselves of every technological resource on the North American continent, but as long as our language is inadequate, our vision remains formless, our thinking and feeling are still running in the old cycles, our process may be "revolutionary" but not transformative.

ADRIENNE RICH

Language makes culture, and we make a rotten culture when we abuse words.

CYNTHIA OZICK

I believe that words *can* help us move or keep us paralyzed, and that our choices of language and verbal tone have something—a great deal—to do with how we live our lives and whom we end up speaking with and hearing; and that we can deflect words, by trivialization, of course, but also by ritualized respect, or we can let them enter our souls and mix with the juices of our minds.

ADRIENNE RICH

The liberation of language is rooted in the liberation of ourselves.

MARY DALY

Language is power, life, and the instrument of domination and liberation.

ANGELA CARTER

Like desire, language disrupts, refuses to be contained within boundaries.

BELL HOOKS

For most women, the language of conversation is primarily a language of rapport: a way of establishing connections and negotiating relationships. . . . For most men, talk is primarily a means to preserve independence and negotiate and maintain status in a hierarchical social order.

DEBORAH TANNEN

Language exerts hidden power, like the moon on the tides.

RITE MAE BROWN

We die. That may be the meaning of life. But we do language. That may be the measure of our lives.

TONI MORRISON

Leaders

Strong people don't need strong leaders.

ELLA BAKER

Do not wait for leaders; do it alone, person to person.

MOTHER TERESA

The secret of a leader lies in the tests he has faced over the whole course of his life and the *habit of action* he develops in meeting those tests.

GAIL SHEEHY

A leader who doesn't hesitate before he sends his nation to battle is not fit to be a leader.

GOLDA MEIR

No leader can be too far ahead of his followers.

ELEANOR ROOSEVELT

It is very hard to be a female leader. While it is assumed that any man, no matter how tough, has a soft side . . . any female leader is assumed to be one-dimensional.

BILLIE JEAN KING

Clearly no one knows what leadership has gone undiscovered in women of all races, and in black and other minority men.

GLORIA STEINEM

We have got to stop the nervous Nellies and the Toms from going to the Man's place. I don't believe in killing, but a good whipping behind the bushes wouldn't hurt them. . . . These bourgeoisie Negroes aren't helping. It's the ghetto Negroes who are leading the way.

FANNIE LOU HAMER

Being prime minister is a lonely job . . . you cannot lead from the crowd.

MARGARET THATCHER

Women have always been the guardians of wisdom and humanity which makes them natural, but usually secret, rulers. The time has come for them to rule openly, but together with and not against men.

CHARLOTTE WOLFF

The failure of women to have reached positions of leadership has been due in large part to social and professional discrimination.

ROSALYN SUSSMAN YALOW

Liberals

The liberals in the House strongly resemble liberals I have known through the last two decades in the civil rights conflict. When it comes time to show on which side they will be counted, they excuse themselves.

SHIRLEY CHISHOLM

No man can call himself liberal, or radical, or even a conservative advocate of fair play, if his work depends in any way on the unpaid or underpaid labor of women at home, or in the office.

GLORIA STEINEM

Long ago, there was a noble word, *liberal*, which derives from the word *free*. Now a strange thing happened to that word. A man named Hitler made it a term of abuse, a matter of suspicion, because those who were not with him were against him, and liberals had no use for Hitler. And then another man named McCarthy cast the same opprobrium on the word. . . .

We must cherish and honor the word *free* or it will cease to apply to us.

ELEANOR ROOSEVELT

Liberal intellectuals ... tend to have a classical theory of politics, in which the state has the monopoly of power; hoping that those in positions of authority may prove to be enlightened men, wielding power justly, they are natural, if cautious, allies of the "establishment."

SUSAN SONTAG

The label of liberalism is hardly a sentence to public ignominy: otherwise Bruce Springsteen would still be rehabilitating used Cadillacs in Asbury Park and Jane Fonda, for all we know, would be just another overweight housewife.

BARBARA EHRENREICH

When Marxist dictators shoot their way into power in Central America, the San Francisco Democrats don't blame the guerrillas and their Soviet allies, they blame United States policies of one hundred years ago, but then they always blame America first.

JEANE KIRKPATRICK

The liberals have not softened their view of actuality to make themselves live closer to the dream, but instead sharpen their perceptions and fight to make the dream actuality or give up the battle in despair.

MARGARET MEAD

Life Lessons

Life loves the liver of it.

MAYA ANGELOU

You have to count on living every single day in a way you believe will make you feel good about your life—so that if it were over tomorrow, you'd be content with yourself.

JANE SEYMOUR

When you realize the value of all life, you dwell less on what is past and concentrate more on the preservation of the future.

DIAN FOSSEY

Take your life in your own hands, and what happens? A terrible thing: no one to blame.

ERICA JONG

It is not true that life is one damn thing after another—it is one damn thing over and over.

EDNA ST. VINCENT MILLAY

What you get is a living—what you give is a life.

LILLIAN GISH

If you want to live on the edge of life, you need to be flexible.

KIM NOVAK

The main dangers in this life are the people who want to change everything—or nothing.

NANCY ASTOR

Life is what we make it, always has been, always will be.

GRANDMA MOSES

We begin life with loss. We are cast from the womb without apartment, a charge plate, a job, or a car.

JUDITH VIORST

Life is something to do when you can't get to sleep.

FRAN LEBOWITZ

Life is not a matter of place, things, or comfort; rather, it concerns the basic human rights of family, country, justice, and human dignity.

IMELDA MARCOS

They sicken of calm, who know the storm.

DOROTHY PARKER

Life is either always a tightrope or a feather bed. Give me the tightrope.

EDITH WHARTON

I don't believe that life is supposed to make you feel good, or to make you feel miserable either. Life is just supposed to make you feel.

GLORIA NAYLOR

It has begun to occur to me that life is a stage I'm going through.

ELLEN GOODMAN

If you really want something you can figure out how to make it happen.

CHER

I have fought and kicked and fasted and prayed and cursed and cried to myself to the point of existing. It has been like being born again, literally. Just *knowing* has meant everything to me. Knowing has pushed me out into the world, into college, into places, into people.

ALICE WALKER

Adventure is worthwhile in itself.

AMELIA EARHART

Death and taxes and childbirth: There's never any convenient time for any of them!

MARGARET MITCHELL

What matters most is that we learn from living.

DORIS LESSING

I wanted a perfect ending. . . . Now I've learned, the hard way, that some poems don't rhyme, and some stories don't have a clear beginning, middle, and end. Life is about not knowing, having to change, taking the moment and making the best of it, without knowing what's going to happen next. Delicious ambiguity.

GILDA RADNER

People create their own questions because they're afraid to look straight. All you have to do is look straight and see the road, and when you see it, don't sit looking at it—walk.

AYN RAND

You must learn day by day, year by year, to broaden your horizon. The more things you love, the more you are interested in, the more you enjoy, the more you are indignant about, the more you have left when anything happens.

ETHEL BARRYMORE

We're all in this alone.

LILY TOMLIN

I like living. I have sometimes been wildly, despairingly, acutely miserable, wracked with sorrow, but through it all I still know quite certainly that just to *be alive* is a grand thing.

AGATHA CHRISTIE

It's going to be a long hard drag, but we'll make it.

JANIS JOPLIN

It's so clear that you have to cherish everyone. I think that's what I get from these older black women, that every soul is to be cherished, that every flower is to bloom.

ALICE WALKER

Life's under no obligation to give us what we expect. We take what we get and are thankful it's no worse than it is.

MARGARET MITCHELL

Too many of us are hung up on what we don't have, can't have, or won't ever have. We spend too much energy being down, when we could use that same energy—if not less of it—doing, or at least trying to do, some of the things we really want to do.

TERRY MCMILLAN

Life is a marvelous, transitory adventure.

NIKKI GIOVANNI

For fast-acting relief try slowing down.

LILY TOMLIN

Limitations

I seldom think about my limitations, and they never make me sad. Perhaps there is just a touch of yearning at times; but it is vague, like a breeze among flowers.

HELEN KELLER

I think knowing what you can *not* do is more important than knowing what you can do. In fact, that's good taste.

LUCILLE BALL

Let's fact it—who ever is adequate? We all create situations each other can't live up to, then break our hearts at them because they don't.

ELIZABETH BOWEN

I'm not going to limit myself just because people won't accept the fact that I can do something else.

DOLLY PARTON

Learning too soon our limitations, we never learn our powers.

MIGNON MCLAUGHLIN

Literature

The novel is a game or joke shared between author and reader.

ANNIE DILLARD

Literature is strewn with the wreckage of men who have minded beyond reason the opinions of others.

VIRGINIA WOOLF

Literature is an instrument of culture, not a summary of it.

CYNTHIA OZICK

Socrates wrote nothing. Christ wrote nothing.

IRISH MURDOCH

Literature is the lie that tells the truth.

DOROTHY ALLISON

There are only two or three human stories, and they go on repeating themselves as fiercely as if they had never happened before.

WILLA CATHER

Literature is analysis after the event.

DORIS LESSING

I don't care very much for literary shrines and haunts . . . I
knew a woman in London who boasted that she had lodgings
from the windows of which she could throw a stone into
Carlyle's yard. And when I said, "Why throw a stone into
Carlyle's yard?" she looked at me as if I were an imbecile and
changed the subject.

CAROLYN WELLS

The illusion of art is to make one believe that great literature
is very close to life, but exactly the opposite is true. Life is
amorphous, literature is formal.

FRANÇOISE SAGAN

I have watched . . . many literary fashions shoot up and
blossom, and then fade and drop. . . . Yet with the many that
I have seen come and go, I have never yet encountered a mode
of thinking that regarded itself as simply a changing fashion,
and not as an infallible approach to the right culture.

ELLEN GLASGOW

Literature is the last banquet between minds.

EDNA O'BRIEN

Literature is my Utopia. Here I am not disfranchised. No
barrier of the sense shuts me out from the sweet, gracious
discourse of my book friends. They talk to me without
embarrassment or awkwardness.

HELEN KELLER

Literature must be seen in terms of the contemporary concern for survival.

LOUISE ERDRICH

Loneliness

For loneliness is but cutting adrift from our moorings and floating out to the open sea; an opportunity for finding ourselves, our real selves, what we are about, where we are heading during our little time on this beautiful earth.

ANNE SHANNON MONROE

Loneliness and the feeling of being unwanted is the most terrible poverty.

MOTHER TERESA

Solitude is one thing and loneliness is another.

MAY SARTON

Loneliness is never more cruel than when it is felt in close propinquity with someone who has ceased to communicate.

GERMAINE GREER

Loneliness is dangerous. It's bad for you to be alone, to be lonely, because if aloneness does not lead to God, it leads to the devil. It leads to self.

JOYCE CAROL OATES

The gift of loneliness is sometimes a radical vision of society or one's people that has not previously been taken into account.

ALICE WALKER

> Birth is the start
> of loneliness
> & loneliness the start
> of poetry.

ERICA JONG

Solitude is the human condition in which I keep myself company. Loneliness comes about when I am alone without being able to split up into the two-in-one, without being able to keep myself company.

HANNAH ARENDT

> Nobody, but nobody
> Can make it out here alone.

MAYA ANGELOU

Love

If love is the answer, could you please rephrase the question?

LILY TOMLIN

It is impossible to repent of love. The sin of love does not exist.

MURIEL SPARK

Love is a fire. But whether it is going to warm your hearth or burn down your house, you can never tell.

JOAN CRAWFORD

If you give your life as a wholehearted response to love, then love will wholeheartedly respond to you.

MARIANNE WILLIAMSON

Brevity may be the soul of wit, but not when someone's saying "I love you." When someone's saying "I love you," he always ought to give you a lot of details: Like, why does he love you? And, how much does he love you? And, when and where did he first begin to love you? Favorable comparisons with all the other women he ever loved are also welcome. And even though he insists it would take forever to count the ways he loves you, let him start counting.

JUDITH VIORST

Love involves a peculiar unfathomable combination of understanding and misunderstanding.

DIANE ARBUS

Love has nothing to do with what you are expecting to get—only with what you are expecting to give—which is everything.

KATHARINE HEPBURN

Love is a fruit in season at all times, and within reach of every hand.

MOTHER TERESA

Love is as strict as acting. If you want to love somebody, stand there and do it. If you don't, don't. There are no other choices.

TYNE DALY

Love is or it ain't. Thin love ain't love at all.

TONI MORRISON

Love is purely a creation of the human imagination. . . . The important example of how the human imagination continually outruns the creature it inhabits.

KATHERINE ANNE PORTER

Love commingled with hate is more powerful than love. Or hate.

JOYCE CAROL OATES

The more you love someone the more he wants from you and the less you have to give since you've already given him your love.

NIKKI GIOVANNI

Love knows no honor; people in love do things that they never thought they'd do and that they've always despised other people for doing. They violate not only their own scruples but their own *style*.

PAULINE KAEL

Love in action is the answer to every problem in our lives and in this world. Love in action is the force that helped us make it to this place, and it's the truth that will set us free.

SUSAN TAYLOR

One of my theories is that men love with their eyes; women love with their ears.

ZSA ZSA GABOR

By the time you swear you're his,
Shivering and sighing,
And he vows his passion is
Infinite, undying—
Lady, make a note of this:
One of you is lying.

DOROTHY PARKER

Fancy lovers never last.

MAXINE HONG KINGSTON

In real love you want the other person's good. In romantic love you want the other person.

MARGARET ANDERSON

We had a lot in common. I loved him and he loved him.

SHELLEY WINTERS

When there is great love there are always miracles.

WILLA CATHER

You know, a heart can be broken, but it keeps on beating, just the same.

FANNIE FLAGG

A man when he is making up to anybody can be cordial and gallant and full of little attentions and altogether charming. But when a man is really in love he can't help looking like a sheep.

AGATHA CHRISTIE

Love is not enough. It must be the foundation, the cornerstone, but not the complete structure. It is much too pliable, too yielding.

BETTE DAVIS

Secretly, we wish anyone we love will think exactly the way we do.

KIM CHERNIN

Love is not all: it is not meat nor
    drink
Nor slumber nor a roof against the
    rain;
Nor yet a floating spar to men that sink.

EDNA ST. VINCENT MILLAY

Love has pride in nothing—but its own humility.

CLARE BOOTHE LUCE

Love is not self-sacrifice, but the most profound assertion of your own needs and values. It is for your *own* happiness that you need the person you love, and that is the greatest compliment, the greatest tribute you can pay to that person.

AYN RAND

Love is something like the clouds that were in the sky before the sun came out. You cannot touch the clouds, you know; but you feel the rain and know how glad the flowers and the thirsty earth are to have it after a hot day. You cannot touch love either; but you feel the sweetness that it pours into everything. Without love you would not be happy or want to play.

ANNIE SULLIVAN

We are told that people stay in love because of chemistry, or because they remain intrigued with each other, because of many kindnesses, because of luck. . . . But part of it has got to be forgiveness and gratefulness. The understanding that, so, you're no bargain, but you love and you are loved. Anyway.

ELLEN GOODMAN

Marriage

Any intelligent woman who reads the marriage contract, and then goes into it, deserves all the consequences.

ISADORA DUNCAN

The more you invest in a marriage, the more valuable it becomes.

AMY GRANT

We all have a childhood dream that when there is love, everything goes like silk, but the reality is that marriage requires a lot of compromise.

RAQUEL WELCH

It has been said that marriage diminishes man, which is often true; but almost always it annihilates woman.

SIMONE DE BEAUVOIR

Never marry a man who hates his mother because he'll end up hating you.

JILL BENNETT

The birth of a child erases all previous marital agreements.

SUSAN CHEEVER

When you see a married couple coming down the street, the one who is two or three steps ahead is the one that's mad.

HELEN ROWLAND

An archaeologist is the best husband any woman can have: the older she gets, the more interested he is in her.

AGATHA CHRISTIE

I've been married to one Marxist and one Fascist, and neither one would take the garbage out.

LEE GRANT

Marrying a man is like buying something you've been admiring for a long time in a shop window. You may love it when you get it home, but it doesn't always go with everything else in the house.

JEAN KERR

Not knowing what's going on with money in marriage is about as smart as a man expecting his wife to do all the discipline of the children and being surprised one day when one of them goes up on a drug rap.

HELEN GURLEY BROWN

I'm in no hurry. In spite of all the worldly pressure for me to have a wedding, I no longer feel what I felt many years ago— that I have to have a man in order to make myself feel whole.

OPRAH WINFREY

I never married because there was no need. I have three pets at home which answer the same purpose as a husband. I have a dog which growls every morning, a parrot which swears all afternoon, and a cat that comes home late at night.

MARIE CORELLI

A successful marriage requires falling in love many times, always with the same person.

MIGNON MCLAUGHLIN

I can't mate in captivity.

GLORIA STEINEM

In Hollywood all marriages are happy. It's trying to live together afterwards that causes all the problems.

SHELLEY WINTERS

The trouble with some women is that they get all excited about nothing—and then marry him.

CHER

A man in love is incomplete until he is married. Then he's finished.

ZSA ZSA GABOR

You cannot belong to anyone else, until you belong to yourself.

PEARL BAILEY

Marriage is insurance for the worst years of your life. During your best years, you don't need a husband.

HELEN GURLEY BROWN

I suppose when they reach a certain age some men are afraid to grow up. It seems the older the men get, the younger their new wives get.

ELIZABETH TAYLOR

The world is chock-full of interesting and curious things. The point of courtship—marriage—is to secure someone with whom you wish to go hand in hand through this source of entertainment, each making discoveries, and then sharing some and merely reporting others.

JUDITH MARTIN (MISS MANNERS)

Marriage is obsolete; a trap for both sexes where, too often, the man becomes a boss and the woman becomes a shrew.

CATHERINE DENEUVE

When people ask me how we've lived past 100, I say, "Honey, we were never married. We never had husbands to worry us to death. . . . In those days, a man expected you to be in charge of a perfect household, to look after his every need. Honey, I wasn't interested."

BESSIE DELANY

Marriage represents the intervention of the state in a love affair which probably wasn't going too well anyway.

MIGNON MCLAUGHLIN

Marriage is a series of desperate arguments people feel passionately about.

KATHARINE HEPBURN

The *divine right* of husbands, like the divine right of kings, may, it is hoped, in the enlightened age, be contested without danger.

MARY WOLLSTONECRAFT

Marriage ain't easy but nothing that's worth much ever is.

LILLIAN CARTER

If there is to be any romance in marriage women must be given every chance to earn a decent living at other occupations. Otherwise no man can be sure that he is loved for himself alone, and that his wife did not come to the Registry Office because she had no luck at the Labor Exchange.

REBECCA WEST

One of the great reasons why so many husbands and wives make shipwrecks of their lives together is because a man is always seeking for happiness, while a woman is on a perpetual still hunt for trouble.

DOROTHY DIX

Marriage is not just spiritual communion and passionate embraces; marriage is also three meals a day, sharing the workload, and remembering to carry out the trash.

DR. JOYCE BROTHERS

Marriage is a job. Happiness or unhappiness has nothing to do with it. There was never a marriage that could not be made a success, nor a marriage that could not have ended in bitterness and failure.

KATHLEEN NORRIS

Marriage is a half step, a way to leave home without losing home.

GAIL SHEEHY

Marriage is a very alienating institution, for men as well as women; it's a very dangerous situation—dangerous for men, who find themselves saddled with wife and children to support; dangerous for women, who aren't financially independent of men who can throw them out when they're forty; and very dangerous for children, because their parents vent all their frustrations and mutual hatred on them. The very words "conjugal rights" are dreadful. Any institution which solders one person to another, obliging people to sleep together who no longer want to, is a bad one.

SIMONE DE BEAUVOIR

A successful marriage is not a gift; it is an achievement.

ANN LANDERS

When a girl marries she exchanges the attentions of many men for the inattention of one.

HELEN ROWLAND

The reason husbands and wives do not understand each other is because they belong to different sexes.

DOROTHY DIX

It is true that I never should have married, but I didn't want to live without a man. Brought up to respect the conventions, love had to end in marriage. I'm afraid it did.

BETTE DAVIS

A lot of men think of their wives as replacing their mothers.

JOYCE BROTHERS

You've got to be willing to stay committed to someone over the long run, and sometimes it doesn't work out. But often if you become real honest with yourself and honest with each other, and put aside whatever personal hurt and disappointment you have to really understand yourself and your spouse, it can be the most wonderful experience you'll ever have.

HILLARY RODHAM CLINTON

If a woman is really injured by her marriage she should sue under the employer liability act. She should claim damages—not alimony.

CHARLOTTE PERKINS GILMAN

Wasn't marriage, like life, unstimulating and unprofitable and somewhat empty when too well ordered and protected and guarded? Wasn't it finer, more splendid, more nourishing, when it was, like life itself, a mixture of the sordid and the magnificent; of mud and stars; of earth and flowers; of love and hate and laughter and tears and ugliness and beauty and hurt?

EDNA FERBER

Memory

Some memories are realities, and are better than anything that can ever happen to one again.

WILLA CATHER

Women forget all the things they don't want to remember, and remember everything they don't want to forget. . . . Then they act and do things accordingly.

ZORA NEALE HURSTON

When you have committed an action that you cannot bear to think about, that causes you to writhe in retrospect, do not seek to evade the memory: make yourself relive it, confront it repeatedly over and over, till finally, you will discover, through sheer repetition it loses its power to pain you. It works, I guarantee you, this surefire guilt-eradicator, like a homeopathic medicine—like in small doses applied to like. It works, but I am not sure that is a good thing.

MARY MCCARTHY

I have always been driven by some distant music—a battle hymn no doubt—for I have been at war from the beginning. I've never looked back before. I've never had the time and it has always seemed so dangerous. To look back is to relax one's vigil.

BETTE DAVIS

What a strange thing memory is, and hope; one looks backward, the other forward. The one is of today, the other is the tomorrow. Memory is history recorded in our brain, memory is a painter, it paints pictures of the past and of the day.

GRANDMA MOSES

The memory . . . experiencing and re-experiencing, has such power over one's mere personal life, that one has merely lived.

REBECCA WEST

The charm, one might say the genius, of memory is that it is choosy, chancy, and temperamental; it rejects the edifying cathedral and indelibly photographs the small boy outside, chewing a hunk of melon in the dust.

ELIZABETH BOWEN

Oh better than the minting
Of a gold-crowned king
Is the safe-kept memory
Of a lovely thing.

SARA TEASDALE

It's a pleasure to share one's memories. Everything remembered is dear, endearing, touching, precious. At least the past is safe—though we don't know it at the time. We know it now. Because it's in the past; because we have survived.

SUSAN SONTAG

Memory is a magnet. It will pull to it and hold only material nature has designed it to attract.

JESSAMYN WEST

Writing fiction has developed in me an abiding respect for the unknown in a human lifetime and a sense of where to look for threads, how to follow, how to connect, find in the thick of the tangle what clear line persists. The strands are all there: to the memory nothing is ever really lost.

EUDORA WELTY

As a life's work, I would remember everything—everything, against loss. I would go through life like a plankton net.

ANNIE DILLARD

All water has a perfect memory and is forever trying to get back to where it was.

TONI MORRISON

Mistakes

A mistake is simply another way of doing things.

KATHARINE GRAHAM

If I had to live my life over again, I'd dare to make more mistakes next time.

NADINE STAIR

Mistakes are part of the dues one pays for a full life.

SOPHIA LOREN

Maybe being oneself is always an acquired taste.

PATRICIA HEMPL

Show me a person who has never made a mistake and I'll show you somebody who has never achieved much.

JOAN COLLINS

The art of never making a mistake is crucial to motherhood. To be effective and to gain the respect she needs to function, a mother must have her children believe she has never engaged in sex, never made a bad decision, never caused her own mother a moment's anxiety, and was never a child.

ERMA BOMBECK

Be bold. If you're going to make an error, make a doozy, and don't be afraid to hit the ball.

BILLIE JEAN KING

If I had to live my life again, I'd make the same mistakes, only sooner.

TALLULAH BANKHEAD

Mistakes are a fact of life. It is the response to error that counts.

NIKKI GIOVANNI

Every great mistake has a halfway moment, a split second when it can be recalled and perhaps remedied.

PEARL S. BUCK

There is no reason to repeat bad history.

ELEANOR HOLMES NORTON

Motherhood

Motherhood is the second oldest profession in the world. . . .
It's the biggest on-the-job training program in existence today.

ERMA BOMBECK

Sometimes the strength of motherhood is greater than natural
laws.

BARBARA KINGSOLVER

There's a lot more to being a woman than being a mother,
but there's a hell of a lot more to being a mother than most
people suspect.

ROSEANNE

You have to love your children unselfishly. That's hard. But
it's the only way.

BARBARA BUSH

Babies don't come with directions on the back or batteries
that can be removed. Motherhood is twenty-four hours a day,
seven days a week. You can't "leave the office."

PATRICIA SCHROEDER

Mother knows best.

EDNA FERBER

When you are a mother, you are never really alone in your thoughts. You are connected to your child and to all those who touch your lives. A mother always has to think twice, once for herself and once for her child.

SOPHIA LOREN

Clever men create themselves, but clever women, it seems to me, are created by their mothers. Women can never quite escape their mothers' cosmic pull, not their lip-biting expectations or their faulty love. We want to please our mothers, emulate them, disgrace them, oblige them, outrage them, and bury ourselves in the mysteries and consolations of their presence.

CAROL SHIELDS

I was happy to have children. . . . I wanted my body, as well as my mind and spirit, to succeed, to reach an appropriate glory.

GWENDOLYN BROOKS

A mother's hardest to forgive.
Life is the fruit she longs to hand you,
Ripe on a plate. And while you live,
Relentlessly she understands you.

PHYLLIS MCGINLEY

To me life is tough enough without having someone kick you from the inside.

RITA RUDNER

Women who miscalculate are called "mothers."

ABIGAIL VAN BUREN

The finest inheritance you can give to a child is to allow it to make its own way, completely on its own feet.

ISADORA DUNCAN

I discovered when I had a child of my own that I had become a biased observer of small children. Instead of looking at them with affectionate but nonpartisan eyes, I saw each of them as older or younger, bigger or smaller, more or less graceful, intelligent, or skilled than my own child.

MARGARET MEAD

My child looked at me and I looked back at him in the delivery room, and I realized that out of a sea of infinite possibilities it had come down to this: a specific person, born on the hottest day of the year, conceived on a Christmas Eve, made by his father and me miraculously from scratch.

ANNA QUINDLEN

It takes a woman twenty years to make a man of her son, and another woman twenty minutes to make a fool of him.

HELEN ROWLAND

Is it possible that my sons-in-law will do toilets? If we raise boys to know that diapers need to be changed and refrigerators need to be cleaned, there's hope for the next generation.

ANNE ROIPHE

The real menace in dealing with a five-year-old is that in no time at all you begin to sound like a five-year-old.

JEAN KERR

Some are kissing mothers and some are scolding mothers, but it is love just the same, and most mothers kiss and scold together.

PEARL S. BUCK

Most mothers are instinctive philosophers.

HARRIET BEECHER STOWE

I looked on child rearing not only as a work of love and duty but as a profession that was fully interesting and challenging as any honorable profession in the world and one that demanded the best that I could bring to it.

ROSE KENNEDY

Love and respect are the most important aspects of parenting, and of all relationships.

JODIE FOSTER

Mother and child, yes, but *sisters* really, against whatever denies us all that we are.

ALICE WALKER

Sons do not need you. They are always out of your reach. Walking strange waters. Their mouths are not made for small and intimate speech. Like the speech of daughters.

PHYLLIS MCGINLEY

Mother as an ideal is unfair in the same manner as woman as a sex object.

LIZ SMITH

Music

Anybody singing the blues is in a deep pit yelling for help.

MAHALIA JACKSON

An unalterable and unquestioned law of the musical world required that the German text of French operas sung by Swedish artists should be translated into Italian for the clearer understanding of English-speaking audiences.

EDITH WHARTON

No composer has yet caught the rhythm of America—it is too mighty for the ears of most. But some day it will gush forth from the great stretches of earth, rain down from the vast sky spaces of stars, and the American will be expressed in some mighty music that will shape its chaos to Harmony.

ISADORA DUNCAN

The judgment of music, like the inspiration for it, must come slow and measured, if it comes with truth.

LILLIAN HELLMAN

A woman's two cents worth is worth two cents in the music business.

LORETTA LYNN

Music melts all the separate parts of our bodies together.

ANAÏS NIN

The secret breathed within
And never spoken, woken
By music; the garlands in
Her hands no one has seen.
She wreathes the air with green
and weaves the stillness in.

MAY SARTON

It had never occurred to me before that music and thinking are so much alike. In fact you could say music is another way of thinking, or maybe thinking is another kind of music.

URSULA K. LE GUIN

Music is not written in red, white, and blue. It is written in the heart's blood of the composer.

NELLIE MELBA

I wish the government would put a tax on pianos for the incompetent.

EDITH SITWELL

Optimism

Keep your face to the sunshine and you cannot see the shadows.

HELEN KELLER

There is hope for all of us. Well, anyway, if you don't die you live through it, day in, day out.

MARY BECKETT

Hope is the feeling you have that the feeling you have isn't permanent.

JEAN KERR

Rosiness is not a worse windowpane than gloomy gray when viewing the world.

GRACE PALEY

Birds sing after a storm; why shouldn't people feel as free to delight in whatever remains to them?

ROSE KENNEDY

Just opening up the door, having this ordinary person fly, says a lot for the future. You can always equate astronauts with explorers who were subsidized. Now you are getting someone going just to observe. And then you'll have the settlers.

CHRISTA MCAULIFFE

There are two kinds of stones, as everyone knows, one of which rolls.

AMELIA EARHART

If you can't change your fate, change your attitude.

AMY TAN

I really do believe I can accomplish a great deal with a big grin. I know some people find that disconcerting, but that doesn't matter.

BEVERLY SILLS

When hope is taken away from the people, moral degeneration follows swiftly after.

PEARL S. BUCK

The way I see it, if you want the rainbow, you gotta put up with the rain.

DOLLY PARTON

It's better to light a candle than to curse the darkness.

ELEANOR ROOSEVELT

Our faith in the present dies out long before our faith in the future.

RUTH BENEDICT

As a woman I have no country. As a woman my country is the whole world.

VIRGINIA WOOLF

Parents

Most of us become parents long before we have stopped being children.

MIGNON MCLAUGHLIN

Parents of young children should realize that few people, and maybe no one, will find their children as enchanting as they do.

BARBARA WALTERS

I had the total attention of both my parents, and was secure in the knowledge of being loved. . . . My memories of falling asleep at night are to the comfortable sound of my parents' voices, voices which conveyed in their tones the message that these two people loved and trusted one another.

JILL KER CONWAY

The need to become a separate self is as urgent as the yearning to merge forever. And as long as we, not our mother, initiate parting, and as long as our mother remains reliably there, it seems possible to risk, and even to revel in, standing alone.

JUDITH VIORST

Our goal as a parent is to give life to our children's learning—to instruct, to teach, to help them develop self-discipline—an ordering of the self from the inside, not imposition from the outside. Any technique that does not give life to a child's learning and leave a child's dignity intact cannot be called discipline—it is punishment, no matter what language it is clothed in.

BARBARA COLOROSO

If we can genuinely honor our mother and father, we are not only at peace with ourselves but we can then give birth to our future.

SHIRLEY MACLAINE

I stopped loving my father a long time ago. What remained was the slavery to a pattern.

ANAÏS NIN

I was my father's daughter. . . . He is dead now and I am a grown woman and still I am my father's daughter. . . . I am many things besides, but I am daddy's girl too and so I will remain—all the way to the old folks' home.

PAULA WEIDEGER

Your responsibility as a parent is not as great as you might imagine. You need not supply the world with the next conqueror of disease or major motion-picture star.

FRAN LEBOWITZ

[Parents] must get across the idea that "I love you always, but sometimes I do not love your behavior."

AMY VANDERBILT

If you have never been hated by your child, you have never been a parent.

BETTE DAVIS

I'm not afraid of too many things, and I got that invincible kind of attitude from [my father].

QUEEN LATIFAH

In the next year or so, my signature will appear on $60 billion of United States currency. More important to me, however, is the signature that appears on my life—the strong, proud, assertive handwriting of a loving father and mother.

U.S. TREASURER

KATHERINE D. ORTEGA

I was not close to my father, but he was very special to me. Whenever I did something as a little girl—learn to swim or act in a school play, for instance—he was fabulous. There would be this certain look in his eyes. It made me feel great.

DIANE KEATON

Mama exhorted her children at every opportunity to "jump at de sun." We might not land on the sun, but at least we would get off the ground.

ZORA NEALE HURSTON

Parents can only give advice or put [children] on the right paths, but the final forming of a person's character lies in their own hands.

ANNE FRANK

My father would pick me up and hold me high in the air. He dominated my life as long as he lived, and was the love of my life for many years after he died.

ELEANOR ROOSEVELT

Parents have become so convinced that educators know what is best for children that they forget that they themselves are really experts.

MARIAN WRIGHT EDELMAN

Pets

All I need to know I learned from my cat.

SUZY BECKER

You enter into a certain amount of madness when you marry a person with pets.

NORA EPHRON

In their sympathies, children feel nearer animals than adults. They frolic with animals, caress them, share with them feelings neither has any words for. Have they ever stroked any adult with the love they bestow on a cat? Hugged any grown-up with the ecstasy they feel when clasping a puppy?

JESSAMYN WEST

Which of us has not been stunned by the beauty of an animal's skin or its flexibility in motion?

MARIANNE MOORE

If I could do anything about the way people behave towards each other, I would, but since I can't I'll stick to the animals.

BRIGITTE BARDOT

We are pretty sure that we and our pets share the same reality, until one day we come home to find that our wistful, intelligent friend who reminds us of our better self has decided a good way to spend the day is to open a box of Brillo pads, unravel a few, distribute some throughout the house, and eat or wear all the rest. And we shake our heads in an inability to comprehend what went wrong here.

MERRILL MARKOE

If a fish is the movement of water embodied, given shape, then a cat is a diagram and pattern of subtle air.

DORIS LESSING

Patriotism

Unless our conception of patriotism is progressive, it cannot hope to embody the real affection and the real interest of the nation.

JANE ADDAMS

As soon as my feet touched China, I became Chinese.

AMY TAN

I'll stay until I'm tired of it. So long as Britain needs me, I shall never be tired of it.

MARGARET THATCHER

I declare before you all that my whole life, whether it be long or short, shall be devoted to your service and the service of our great Imperial family to which we all belong.

QUEEN ELIZABETH
(AS PRINCESS ELIZABETH)

I don't mind if my life goes in the service of the nation. If I die, every drop of my blood will invigorate the nation.

INDIRA GANDHI

Together, hand in hand, with our matches and our necklaces, we shall liberate this country.

WINNIE MANDELA

I am secretly afraid of animals. . . . I think it is because of the *usness* in their eyes, with the underlying *not-usness* which belies it, and is so tragic a reminder of the lost age when we human beings branched off and left them: left them to eternal inarticulateness and slavery. Why? their eyes seem to ask.

EDITH WHARTON

I think one reason we admire cats, those of us who do, is their proficiency in one-upmanship. They always seem to come out on top, no matter what they are doing—or pretend they do. Rarely do you see a cat discomfited. They have no conscience, and they never regret. Maybe we secretly envy them.

BARBARA WEBSTER

Poetry

Good poetry and successful revolution change our lives. And you cannot compose a good poem or wage a revolution without changing consciousness unless you attack the language that you share with your enemies and invent a language that you share with your allies.

JUNE JORDAN

For women, poetry is not a luxury. It is a vital necessity of our existence. It forms the quality of the light within which we predicate our hopes and dreams toward survival and change, first made into language, then into idea, then into more tangible action. Poetry is the way we help give name to the nameless so it can be thought. The farthest horizons of our hopes and fears are cobbled by our poems, carved from the rock experiences of our daily lives.

AUDRE LORDE

Poetry is, above all, an approach to the truth of feeling. . . . A fine poem will seize your imagination intellectually—that is, when you reach it, you will reach it intellectually too—but the way is through emotion, through what we call feeling.

MURIEL RUKEYSER

Poetry, the genre of purest beauty, was born of a truncated woman: her head severed from her body with a sword, a symbolic penis.

ANDREA DWORKIN

Poetry is where the language is renewed.

MARGARET ATWOOD

We tend to be so bombarded with information, and we move so quickly, that there's a tendency to treat everything on the surface level and process things quickly. This is antithetical to the kind of openness and perception you have to have to be receptive to poetry. . . . Poetry seems to exist in a parallel universe outside daily life in America.

RITA DOVE

Poetry is the most mistaught subject in any school because we teach poetry by form and not by content.

NIKKI GIOVANNI

Prose—it might be speculated—is discourse; poetry ellipsis. Prose is spoken aloud; poetry overheard.

JOYCE CAROL OATES

I see no reason for calling my work poetry except that there is no other category in which to put it.

MARIANNE MOORE

Poetry is above all a concentration of the *power* of language, which is the power of our ultimate relationship to everything in the universe.

ADRIENNE RICH

Poets

I am an ordinary human being who is impelled to write poetry. . . . I still do feel that a poet has a duty to words, and that words can do wonderful things, and it's too bad to just let them lie there without doing anything with and for them.

GWENDOLYN BROOKS

I would venture to guess that Anon, who wrote so many poems without signing them, was often a woman.

VIRGINIA WOOLF

Poets . . . are the only ones to whom love is not only a crucial, but an indispensable experience, which entitles them to mistake it for a universal one.

HANNAH ARENDT

To a poet the human community is like the community of birds to a bird, singing to each other. Love is one of the reasons we are singing to one another, love of language itself, love of sound, love of singing itself, and love of the other birds.

SHARON OLDS

The poet must be free to love or hate as the spirit moves him, free to change, free to be a chameleon, free to be an *enfant terrible*. He must above all never worry about his effect on other people. Power requires that one do just that all the time. Power requires that the inner person never be unmasked. No, we poets have to go naked. And since this is so, it is better that we stay private people; a naked public person would be rather ridiculous, what?

MAY SARTON

I notice that a great many poets emerge from motherless childhoods. They are either early orphans or their mothers are not mentioned at all. It is not so amazing that many of these same artists turned out to be hounded by depression, drugs, and insanity, but did being motherless also drive them to creativity?

LIZ SMITH

Politics

Ninety-eight percent of the adults in this country are decent, hard-working Americans. It's the other lousy two percent that get all the publicity. But then—we elected them.

LILY TOMLIN

The most radical revolutionary will become a conservative the day after the revolution.

HANNAH ARENDT

The reason there are so few female politicians is that it is too much to put makeup on two faces.

MAUREEN MURPHY

I asked a man in prison once how he happened to be there and he said he had stolen a pair of shoes. I told him if he had stolen a railroad he would be a United States Senator.

MOTHER JONES

A politician ought to be born a foundling and remain a bachelor.

LADY BIRD JOHNSON

It's useless to hold a person to anything he says while he's in love, drunk, or running for office.

SHIRLEY MACLAINE

I must say acting was good training for the political life which lay ahead for us.

NANCY REAGAN

In politics if you want anything said, ask a man. If you want anything done, ask a woman.

MARGARET THATCHER

Some members of the Congress are the best actors in the world.

SHIRLEY CHISHOLM

The First Lady is an unpaid public servant elected by one person—her husband.

LADY BIRD JOHNSON

The key to security is public information. Before you can become a statesman you first have to get elected, and to get elected you have to be a politician pledging support for what the voters want.

MARGARET CHASE SMITH

When people ask me why I am running as a woman, I always answer, "What choice do I have?"

PATRICIA SCHROEDER

I had already learned from more than a decade of political life that I was going to be criticized for something I wanted to do. (If I had spent all day "pouring tea," I would have been criticized for that too.)

ROSALYNN CARTER

The new women in politics seem to be saying that we already know how to lose, thank you very much. Now we want to learn how to win.

GLORIA STEINEM

Prejudice

Of my two "handicaps," being female put many more obstacles in my path than being black.

SHIRLEY CHISHOLM

Racism cannot be separated from capitalism.

ANGELA DAVIS

Mumbling obeisance to the abhorrence of apartheid [is] like those lapsed believers who cross themselves when entering a church.

NADINE GORDIMER

The first problem for all of us, men and women, is not to learn, but to unlearn.

GLORIA STEINEM

The mind that doggedly insists on prejudice often has not intelligence enough to change.

PEARL S. BUCK

When indeed shall we learn that we are all related one to the other, that we are all members of one body? Until the spirit of love for our fellowman, regardless of race, color or creed, shall fill the world, making real in our lives and our deeds the actuality of human brotherhood—until the great mass of the people shall be filled with the sense of responsibility for each other's welfare, social justice can never be attained.

HELEN KELLER

The sharing of joy, whether physical, emotional, psychic or intellectual, forms a bridge between the sharers which can be the basis for understanding much of what is not shared between them, and lessens the threat of their difference.

AUDRE LORDE

Sometimes, I feel discriminated against, but it does not make me angry. It merely astonishes me. How *can* any deny themselves the pleasure of my company. It's beyond me.

ZORA NEALE HURSTON

Race

Being black does not stop you. You can sit out in the world and say, "Well, white people kept me back, and I can't do this." Not so. You can have anything you want if you make up your mind and you want it.

CLARA MCBRIDE HALE

I am who I am *because* I'm a black female.... When I was health director in Arkansas ... I could talk about teenage pregnancy, about poverty, ignorance, and enslavement and how the white power structure had imposed it—*only* because I was a black female. I mean, black people would have eaten up a white male who said what I did.

JOYCELYN ELDERS

I knew someone had to take the first step and I made up my mind not to move.

ROSA PARKS

I do not feel inhibited or bound by what I am. That does not mean that I have never had bad scenes relating to being black and/or a woman, it means that other people's craziness has not managed to make me crazy.

LUCILLE CLIFTON

Black people have been traumatized and psychically wounded. This is something we cannot discuss enough at this historical moment.

BELL HOOKS

Whereas black people can call each other "nigger" with impunity, a white person may not presume to do so unless he doesn't mind dying.

CYNTHIA HEIMEL

I deplore any action which denies artistic talent an opportunity to express itself because of prejudice against race origin.

BESS TRUMAN

As a country, we are in a state of denial about issues of race and racism. And too many of our leaders have concluded that the way to remedy racism is to simply stop talking about race.

LANI GUINIER

When I was a child, it did not occur to me, even once, that the black in which I was encased (I called it brown in those days) would be considered, one day, beautiful. Considered beautiful and called beautiful by great groups.

GWENDOLYN BROOKS

Black women have not historically stood in the pulpit, but that doesn't undermine the fact that they built the churches and maintain the pulpits.

MAYA ANGELOU

But I am not tragically colored. There is no great sorrow damned up in my soul, nor lurking behind my eyes. I do not mind at all. I do not belong to the sobbing school of Negrohood who hold that nature somehow has given them a lowdown dirty deal and whose feelings are hurt about it. . . . No, I do not weep at the world—I am too busy sharpening my oyster knife.

ZORA NEALE HURSTON

We are concerned not only about the Negro poor, but the poor all over America and all over the world. Every man deserves a right to a job or an income so that he can pursue liberty, life, and happiness.

CORETTA SCOTT KING

Black woman—the only legitimate Cinderella in modern America, complete with head rag, broom, and being left to make your own damned dress for a ball you'll have to crash.

GLORIA NAYLOR

If you are going to think black, think positive about it. Don't think down on it, or think it is something in your way. And this way, when you really do want to stretch out, and express how beautiful black is, everybody will hear you . . . How can you not stand tall?—Because you are saying who you are.

LEONTYNE PRICE

Until my singing made me famous, I'd lived so far inside the colored people's world that I didn't have to pay attention every day to the way some white people in this country act toward a person with a darker skin.

MAHALIA JACKSON

I'm just an average citizen. Many black people before me were arrested for defying the bus laws. They prepared the way.

ROSA PARKS

There is an incredible amount of magic and feistiness in black men that nobody has been able to wipe out. But everybody has tried.

TONI MORRISON

Reading

Just the knowledge that a good book is waiting one at the end of the day makes that day happier.

KATHLEEN NORRIS

To me, nothing can be more important than giving children books. It's better to be giving books to children than drug treatment to them when they're fifteen years old. Did it ever occur to anyone that if you put nice libraries in public schools you wouldn't have to put them in prisons?

FRAN LEBOWITZ

Are there not some pursuits that we practice because they are good in themselves, and some pleasures that are final? And is not [reading] among them? I have sometimes dreamt, at least, that when the Day of Judgment dawns and the great conquerors and lawyers and statesmen come to receive their rewards . . . the Almighty will turn to Peter and say, not without a certain envy when He sees us coming with our books under our arms, "Look, these need no reward. We have nothing to give them here. They have loved reading."

VIRGINIA WOOLF

The unread story is not a story; it is little black marks on wood pulp. The reader, reading it, makes it live: a live thing, a story.

URSULA K. LE GUIN

Only one hour in a day is more pleasurable than the hour spent in bed with a book before going to sleep, and that is the hour spent in bed with a book after being called in the morning.

ROSE MACAULAY

A bit of trash now and then is good for the severest reader. It provides that necessary roughage in the literary diet.

PHYLLIS MCGINLEY

The pleasure of all reading is doubled when one lives with another who shares the same books.

KATHERINE MANSFIELD

Reading a book is like re-writing it for yourself. . . . You bring to a novel, anything you read, all your experiences of the world. You bring your history and you read it in your own terms.

ANGELA CARTER

Reality

If someone tells you he is going to make a "realistic decision," you immediately understand that he has resolved to do something bad.

MARY MCCARTHY

Reality is something you rise above.

LIZA MINNELLI

Because I and my reality did not comport with what they accepted as their reality, I and my reality had to be reconstructed by the Senate committee members with assistance from the press and others.

ANITA HILL

Reality was such a jungle—with no signposts, landmarks, or boundaries.

HELEN HAYES

Parables are unnecessary for recognizing the blatant absurdity of everyday life. Reality is lesson enough.

JANE O'REILLY

Reality is above all else a variable, and nobody is qualified to say that he or she knows exactly what it is. As a matter of fact, with a firm enough commitment, you can sometimes create a reality which did not exist before.

MARGARET HALSEY

The greatest mystery is in unsheathed reality itself.

EUDORA WELTY

The ordinary is simply the universal observed from the surface, that the direct approach to reality is not without, but within. Touch life anywhere . . . and you will touch universality wherever you touch the earth.

ELLEN GLASGOW

The human mind can bear plenty of reality, but not too much intermittent gloom.

MARGARET DRABBLE

Some people are still unaware that reality contains unparalleled beauties. The fantastic and unexpected, the ever-changing and renewing is nowhere so exemplified as in real life itself.

BERENICE ABBOTT

Regrets

The bitterest tears shed over graves are for words left unsaid and deeds left undone.

HARRIET BEECHER STOWE

Make it a rule of life never to regret and never look back. We all live in suspense, from day to day, from hour to hour; in other words, we are the hero of our own story.

MARY MCCARTHY

Regret is an appalling waste of energy; you can't build on it; it's only good for wallowing in.

KATHERINE MANSFIELD

I have loved badly, loved the great
Too soon, withdrawn my words too late;
And eaten in an echoing hall
Alone and from a chipped plate
The words that I withdrew too late.

EDNA ST. VINCENT MILLAY

Only in your imagination can you revise.

FAY WRAY

I have no regrets. I wouldn't have lived my life the way I did if I was going to worry about what people were going to say.

INGRID BERGMAN

Should-haves solve nothing. It's the next thing to happen that
needs thinking about.
ALEXANDRA RIPLEY

Relationships

Men and women, women and men. It will never work.
ERICA JONG

The most important thing in a relationship between a man
and a woman is that one of them be good at taking orders.
LINDA FESTA

A woman has got to love a bad man once or twice in her life
to be thankful for a good one.
MARJORIE KINNAN RAWLINGS

A date, at this juncture in history, is any prearranged meeting
with a member of the opposite sex toward whom you have
indecent intentions. . . . One does not have to sleep with, or
even touch, someone who has paid for your meal. All those
obligations are hereby rendered null and void, and any man
who doesn't think so needs a quick jab in the kidney.
CYNTHIA HEIMEL

We measure success and depth by length of time, but it is possible to have a deep relationship that doesn't always stay the same.

BARBARA HERSHEY

The easiest kind of relationship for me is with ten thousand people. The hardest is with one.

JOAN BAEZ

Ideally, couples need three lives; one for him, one for her, and one for them together.

JACQUELINE BISSET

What is exciting is not for one person to be stronger than the other . . . but for two people to have met their match and yet they are equally as stubborn, as obstinate, as passionate, as crazy as the other.

BARBRA STREISAND

When we describe what the other person is really like, I suppose we often picture what we want. We look through the prism of our need.

ELLEN GOODMAN

A good woman inspires a man; a brilliant woman interests him; a beautiful woman fascinates him; and a sympathetic woman gets him.

HELEN ROWLAND

When two people love each other, they don't look at each other, they look in the same direction.

GINGER ROGERS

It serves me right for putting all my eggs in one bastard.

DOROTHY PARKER

The biggest mistake is believing there is one right way to listen, to talk, to have a conversation—or a relationship.

DEBORAH TANNEN

In a great romance, each person basically plays a part that the other one really likes.

ELIZABETH ASHLEY

There are men I could spend eternity with. But not this life.

KATHLEEN NORRIS

Woman's life must be wrapped up in a man, and the cleverest woman on earth is the biggest fool with a man.

DOROTHY PARKER

Sometimes I wonder if men and women really suit each other. Perhaps they should live next door and just visit now and then.

KATHARINE HEPBURN

Never go to bed mad. Stay up and fight.

PHYLLIS DILLER

Anger repressed can poison a relationship as surely as the cruelest words.

JOYCE BROTHERS

I never liked the men I loved, and I never loved the men I liked.

FANNY BRICE

New links must be forged as old ones rust.

JANE HOWARD

I don't need an overpowering, powerful, rich man to feel secure. I'd much rather have a man who is there for me, who really loves me, who is growing, who is real.

BIANCA JAGGER

Personally, I think if a woman hasn't met the right man by the time she's 24, she may be lucky.

JEAN KERR

The hardest task in a girl's life is to prove to a man that his intentions are serious.

HELEN ROWLAND

When he is late for dinner and I know he must be either having an affair or lying dead in the street, I always hope he's dead.

JUDITH VIORST

Religion

I think it pisses God off if you walk by the color purple in a field somewhere and don't notice it.

ALICE WALKER

Jesus died for somebody's sins but not mine.

PATTI SMITH

When we talk to God, we're praying. When God talks to us, we're schizophrenic.

LILY TOMLIN

A religious awakening which does not awaken the sleeper to love has roused him in vain.

JESSAMYN WEST

I can't see (or feel) the conflict between love and religion. To me they're the same thing.

ELIZABETH BOWEN

Religion is a superstition that originated in man's mental inability to solve natural phenomena. The Church is an organized institution that has always been a stumbling block to progress.

EMMA GOLDMAN

I was liberated but not too liberated. I was Catholic, you see, and my conscience always bothered me.

EILEEN O'CASEY

There is but one love of Jesus, as there is but one person in the poor—Jesus. We take vows of chastity to love Christ with undivided love; to be able to love him with undivided love we take a vow of poverty which frees us from all material possessions, and with that freedom we can love him with undivided love, and from this vow of undivided love we surrender ourselves totally to him in the person who takes his place.

MOTHER TERESA

Christianity really is a man's religion: there's not much in it for women except docility, obedience, who-sweeps-a-room-as-for-thy-cause, downcast eyes, and death in childbirth. For the men it's better: all power and money and fine robes, the burning of heretics—fun, fun, fun!—and the Inquisition fulminating from the pulpit.

FAY WELDON

I would not attack the faith of a heathen without being sure I had a better one to put in its place.

HARRIET BEECHER STOWE

My ancestors wandered lost in the wilderness for forty years because even in biblical times, men would not stop to ask for directions.

ELAYNE BOOSLER

Self

I never loved a person the way I loved myself.

MAE WEST

No one can make you feel inferior without your consent.

ELEANOR ROOSEVELT

Would that there were an award for people who come to understand the concept of enough. Good enough. Successful enough. Thin enough. Rich enough. Socially responsible enough. When you have self-respect you have enough, and when you have enough, you have self-respect.

GAIL SHEEHY

I was always looking outside myself for strength and confidence but it comes from within. It is there all the time.

ANNA FREUD

The willingness to accept responsibility for one's own life is the source from which self-respect springs.

JOAN DIDION

You have got to discover you, what you do, and trust it.

BARBRA STREISAND

To say something nice about themselves, this is the hardest thing in the world for people to do. They'd rather take their clothes off.

NANCY FRIDAY

I love myself when I am laughing. And then again when I am looking mean and impressive.

ZORA NEALE HURSTON

Love yourself first and everything else falls into line. You really have to love yourself to get anything done in this world.

LUCILLE BALL

The events in our lives happen in a sequence in time, but in their significance to ourselves, they find their own order . . . the continuous thread of revelation.

EUDORA WELTY

The delights of self-discovery are always available.

GAIL SHEEHY

I have often wished I had time to cultivate modesty. . . . But I am too busy thinking about myself.

DAME EDITH SITWELL

Let me listen to me and not to them.

GERTRUDE STEIN

We have to dare to be ourselves, however frightening or strange that self may prove to be.

MAY SARTON

It was on the road and at that hour that I first became aware of my own self, experienced an inexpressible state of grace, and felt one with the first breath of air that stirred, the first bird, and the sun so newly born that it still looked not quite round.

COLETTE

Women are always being tested . . . but ultimately, each of us has to define who we are individually and then do the very best job we can to grow into that.

HILLARY RODHAM CLINTON

Who I am is the best I can be.

LEONTYNE PRICE

Your thorns are the best part of you.

MARIANNE MOORE

I was raised to sense what someone wanted me to be and be that kind of person. It took me a long time not to judge myself through someone else's eyes.

SALLY FIELD

To be one woman, truly, wholly, is to be all women. Tend one garden and you will birth worlds.

KATE BRAVERMAN

Let the world know you as you are, not as you think you should be, because sooner or later, if you are posing, you will forget the pose, and then where are you?

FANNY BRICE

I don't need a man to rectify my existence. The most profound relationship we'll ever have is the one with ourselves.

SHIRLEY MACLAINE

She had nothing to fall back on; not maleness, not whiteness, not ladyhood, not anything. And out of the profound desolation of her reality she may well have invented herself.

TONI MORRISON

There's a period of life when we swallow a knowledge of ourselves and it becomes either good or sour inside.

PEARL BAILEY

Sex

Men reach their sexual peak at eighteen. Women reach theirs at thirty-five. Do you get the feeling God is playing a practical joke?

RITA RUDNER

Woody Allen was right when someone asked him if he thought sex was dirty and he said, "If you do it right." Sex is not some sort of pristine, reverent ritual. You want reverent and pristine, go to church.

CYNTHIA HEIMEL

In my sex fantasy, nobody ever loves me for my mind.

NORA EPHRON

Sex is hardly ever just about sex.

SHIRLEY MACLAINE

Anyone who's a great kisser I'm always interested in.

CHER

The man takes a body that is not his, claims it, sows his so-called seed, reaps a harvest—he colonizes a female body, robs it of its natural resources, controls it.

ANDREA DWORKIN

I'm pure as the driven slush.

TALLULAH BANKHEAD

Sex is perhaps like culture—a luxury that only becomes an art after generations of leisurely acquaintance.

ALICE B. TOKLAS

Don't bother discussing sex with small children. They rarely have anything to add.

FRAN LEBOWITZ

I had the feeling that Pandora's box contained the mysteries of woman's sensuality, so different from man's and for which man's language was inadequate. The language of sex had yet to be invented.

ANAÏS NIN

Girls who put out are tramps. Girls who don't are ladies. This is, however, a rather archaic use of the word. Should one of you boys happen upon a girl who doesn't put out, do not jump to the conclusion that you have found a lady. What you have probably found is a lesbian.

FRAN LEBOWITZ

I used to be a virgin, but I gave it up because there was no money in it.

MARSHA WARFIELD

When you look back at your life . . . what you really find out is that the only person you really go to bed with is yourself.

SHIRLEY MACLAINE

You mustn't force sex to do the work of love or love to do the work of sex.

MARY MCCARTHY

I don't want to see any faces at this party I haven't sat on.

BONNIE RAITT

The prerequisite for making love is to like someone enormously.

HELEN GURLEY BROWN

If men knew what women laughed about, they would never sleep with us.

ERICA JONG

Sex when you're married is like going to a 7-Eleven. There's not much variety, but at three in the morning it's always there.

CAROL LEIFER

Sexual Attraction

Infatuation is when you think that he's as sexy as Robert Redford, as smart as Henry Kissinger, as noble as Ralph Nader, as funny as Woody Allen and as athletic as Jimmy Connors. Love is when you realize that he's as sexy as Woody Allen, as smart as Jimmy Connors, as funny as Ralph Nader, as athletic as Henry Kissinger and nothing like Robert Redford—but you'll take him anyway.

JUDITH VIORST

It's always the mind with me—I don't care if the guy looks like a bowling ball.

SHIRLEY MACLAINE

I have so little sex appeal that my gynecologist calls me "sir."

JOAN RIVERS

A man who insists he never has a twinge of desire for another woman, never fantasizes about other women, and lusts only for his wife—after twenty years of marriage, mind you—is, in my opinion, a phoney.

HELEN GURLEY BROWN

Sex appeal is fifty percent what you've got and fifty percent what people think you've got.

SOPHIA LOREN

The flip side to being attracted to unavailable people is how bored you are by available people. Available people are terrifying because they want to hang around long enough to know you, to like you, to accept you. The problem is not that you attract unavailable people—the problem is that you give them your number.

MARIANNE WILLIAMSON

No one knows how it is that with one glance a boy can break through into a girl's heart.

NANCY THAYER

Tell me what a man finds sexually attractive and I will tell you his entire philosophy of life.

AYN RAND

There are some men who possess a quality which goes way beyond romantic or even sexual appeal, a quality that literally enslaves. It has very little to do with looks and nothing at all to do with youth, because there are some quite mature and unathletic specimens who have it. It's an expression in the eyes, or an aura of being in control, and responsible, or something easy and powerful in the stance, or who knows.

LUCILLE KALLEN

The only place men want depth in a woman is in her décolletage.

ZSA ZSA GABOR

Men aren't attracted to me by my mind. They're attracted by what I don't mind.

GYPSY ROSE LEE

Singers

I see their souls, and I hold them in my hands, and because I love them they weigh nothing.

PEARL BAILEY ON AUDIENCES

For me, singing sad songs often has a way of healing a situation. It gets the hurt out in the open—into the light, out of the darkness.

REBA MCENTIRE

I can hold a note as long as the Chase Manhattan Bank.

ETHEL MERMAN

To sing is to love and to affirm, to fly and soar, to coast into the hearts of the people who listen, to tell them that life is to live, that love is there, that nothing is a promise, but that beauty exists, and must be hunted for and found. That death is a luxury, better to be romanticized and sung about than dwelt upon in the fact of life.

JOAN BAEZ

I can't stand to sing the same song the same way two nights in succession, let alone two years or ten years. If you can, then it ain't music, it's close-order drill or exercise or yodeling or something, not music.

BILLIE HOLIDAY

I consider myself a spokesperson for women all over America, all over the world because no matter what color you are, every woman has experienced what I'm singing about.

TONI BRAXTON

I have, on occasion, sacrificed myself and my own emotional makeup, singing "I'm selfish and I'm sad," for instance. These are not attractive things in the context of rock 'n' roll—which is "Honey, I'm a lover and I'm bad!"

JONI MITCHELL

There are two kinds of talent, man-made talent and God-given talent. With man-made talent you have to work very hard. With God-given talent, you just touch it up once in a while.

PEARL BAILEY

Singlehood

I earn and pay my own way as a great many women do today. Why should unmarried women be discriminated against— unmarried men are not.

DINAH SHORE

I'm single because I was born that way.

MAE WEST

I love being single. It's almost like being rich.

SUE GRAFTON

Surely even those immune from the world . . . need the touch of another. . . .

EUDORA WELTY

Once you have lived with another, it is a great torture to have to live alone.

CARSON MCCULLERS

Being an old maid is like death by drowning, a really delightful sensation after you cease to struggle.

EDNA FERBER

I had reconciled myself to a life without marriage or children for the sake of my career. And then my brothers got married. I realized I didn't even have a home, that in the future I couldn't do politics when I had to ask permission from their wives as to whether I could use the dining room or the telephone. I couldn't rent a home because a woman living on her own can be suspected of all kinds of scandalous associations. So keeping in mind that many people in Pakistan looked to me, I decided to make a personal sacrifice in what I thought would be, more or less, a loveless marriage, a marriage of convenience.

BENAZIR BHUTTO

Sleep

I did not sleep. I never do when I am over-happy, over-unhappy, or in bed with a strange man.

EDNA O'BRIEN

No day is so bad it can't be fixed with a nap.

CARRIE SNOW

How do people go to sleep? I'm afraid I've lost the knack. I might try busting myself smartly over the temple with the night-light. I might repeat to myself, slowly and soothingly, a list of quotations beautiful from minds profound; if I can remember any of the damn things.

DOROTHY PARKER

Most people spend their lives going to bed when they're not sleepy and getting up when they are!

CINDY ADAMS

Sleeping alone, except under doctor's orders, does much harm. Children will tell you how lonely it is sleeping alone. If possible you should always sleep with someone you love. You both recharge your mutual batteries free of charge.

MARLENE DIETRICH

Sleep is death without the responsibility.

FRAN LEBOWITZ

Society

Civilization is a method of living, an attitude of equal respect for all men.

JANE ADDAMS

You cannot hope to build a better world without improving the individuals. To that end each of us must work for his own improvement, and at the same time share a general responsibility for all humanity, our particular duty being to aid those to whom we think we can be most useful.

MARIE CURIE

The truth is that Mozart, Pascal, Boolean algebra, Shakespeare, parliamentary government, baroque churches, Newton, the emancipation of women, Kant, Marx, Balanchine ballet *et al.*, don't redeem what this particular civilization has wrought upon the world. The white race *is* the cancer of human history, it is the white race, and it alone—its ideologies and inventions—which eradicates autonomous civilizations wherever it spreads, which has upset the ecological balance of the planet, which now threatens the very existence of life itself.

SUSAN SONTAG

There is no such thing as society. There are individual men and women, and there are families.

MARGARET THATCHER

Women are the architects of society.

HARRIET BEECHER STOWE

If our American way of life fails the child, it fails us all.

PEARL S. BUCK

I say that if each person in this world will simply take a small piece of this huge thing, this tablecloth, bedspread, whatever, and work on it regardless of the color of the yarn, we will have harmony on this planet.

CICELY TYSON

I am for lifting everyone off the social bottom. In fact, I am for doing away with the social bottom altogether.

CLARE BOOTHE LUCE

What most people don't seem to realize is that there is just as much money to be made out of the wreckage of civilization as from the upbuilding of one.

MARGARET MITCHELL

The critical responsibility for the generation you're in is to help provide the shoulders, the direction, and the support for those generations who come behind.

GLORIA DEAN RANDLE SCOTT

If we are to achieve a richer culture—one rich in contrasting values—we must recognize the whole gamut of human potentialities, and so weave a less arbitrary social fabric, one in which each diverse human gift will find a fitting place.

MARGARET MEAD

Solitude

What a lovely surprise to discover how un-lonely being alone can be.

ELLEN BURSTYN

What a commentary on civilization, when being alone is considered suspect; when one has to apologize for it, make excuses, hide the fact that one practices it—like a secret vice.

ANNE MORROW LINDBERGH

It's like magic. When you live by yourself, all your annoying habits are gone!

MERRILL MARKOE

She would not exchange her solitude for anything. Never again to be forced to move to the rhythms of others.

TILLIE OLSEN

Inside myself is a place where I live alone and that's where you renew your springs that never dry up.

PEARL S. BUCK

Solitude is my element, and the reason is that extreme awareness of other people (all naturally solitary people must feel this) precludes awareness of one's self so after a while the self no longer knows it exists.

MAY SARTON

The human animal needs a freedom seldom mentioned, freedom from intrusion. He needs a little privacy quite as much as he wants understanding of vitamins or exercise or praise.

PHYLLIS MCGINLEY

I restore myself when I'm alone. A career is born in public— talent in privacy.

MARILYN MONROE

Solitude is un-American.

SUSAN SONTAG

When alone I am not aware of my race or my sex, both in need of social contexts for definition.

MAXINE HONG KINGSTON

Certain springs are tapped only when we are alone. . . . Women need solitude in order to find again the true essence of themselves; that firm strand which will be the indispensable center of a whole web of human relationships.

ANNE MORROW LINDBERGH

Spirituality

People see God every day. They just don't recognize him.

PEARL BAILEY

The spirit can split the sky in two and let the face of God
shine through.

EDNA ST. VINCENT MILLAY

The religious need of the human mind remains alive, never
more so, but it demands a teaching which can be *understood*.
Slowly an apprehension of the intimate, usable power of God
is growing among us, and a growing recognition of the only
worthwhile application of that power—in the improvement of
the world.

CHARLOTTE PERKINS GILMAN

The shortness of time, the certainty of death, and the
instability of all things here induce me to turn my thoughts
from earth to heaven.

MARIA W. STEWART

It is not my business to think about myself. My business is to
think about God. It is for God to think about me.

SIMONE WEIL

The power to love what is purely abstract is given to few.

MARGOT ASQUITH

Spirit is an invisible force made visible in all life.

MAYA ANGELOU

Sports

Generally speaking, I look upon [sports] as dangerous and tiring activities performed by people with whom I share nothing except the right to trial by jury.
>   FRAN LEBOWITZ

If a man watches three football games in a row, he should be declared legally dead.
>   ERMA BOMBECK

Well, they're southern people, and if they know you are working at home, they think nothing of walking right in for coffee. But they wouldn't dream of interrupting you at golf.
>   HARPER LEE,
>   ON WHY SHE HAS DONE HER BEST CREATIVE
>   THINKING WHILE PLAYING GOLF

Boxing has become America's tragic theater.
>   JOYCE CAROL OATES

In the field of sports you are more or less accepted for what you do rather than what you are.
>   ALTHEA GIBSON

Stuffed deer heads on walls are bad enough, but it's worse when they are wearing dark glasses and have streamers and ornaments in their antlers because then you know they were enjoying themselves at a party when they were shot.

ELLEN DEGENERIS

You've got to win in sports—that's talent—but you've also got to learn how to remind everybody how you did win, and how often. That comes with experience.

BILLIE JEAN KING

Freedom to explore our environment and develop our bodily abilities is a link to intellectual development.

GLORIA STEINEM

The new female consciousness that has developed over the last decade extends to our right to physical as well as economic, political and social equality. We not only need to develop and extend our physical limits, we want to. And we refuse to be afraid that we will no longer be considered attractive and acceptable when we are strong. We now recognize the strong, healthy woman who has fulfilled her physical potential, as beautiful.

JANE FONDA

Struggle

Trouble is a part of your life, and if you don't share it, you don't give the person who loves you a chance to love you enough.

DINAH SHORE

Walk away from it until you're stronger. All your problems will be there when you get back, but you'll be better able to cope.

LADY BIRD JOHNSON

A woman is like a teabag; you never know how strong she is until she gets in hot water.

NANCY REAGAN

In his own way each man must struggle, lest the normal law become a far-off abstraction utterly separated from his active life.

JANE ADDAMS

Those who have suffered understand suffering and therefore extend their hand.

PATTI SMITH

Our way is not soft grass, it's a mountain path with lots of rocks. But it goes upwards, forward, toward the sun.

RUTH WESTHEIMER

Parents learn a lot from their children about coping with life.
MURIEL SPARK

Whatever you do, don't give up. Because all you can do once you've given up is bitch. I've known some great bitchers in my time. With some it's a passion, with others an art.
MOLLY IVINS

If we had no winter, the spring would not be so pleasant:
If we did not sometimes taste of adversity, prosperity
would not be so welcome.
ANNE BRADSTREET

No life is so hard that you can't make it easier by the way you take it.
ELLEN GLASGOW

You may have to fight a battle more than once to win it.
MARGARET THATCHER

You can't be brave if you've only had wonderful things happen to you.
MARY TYLER MOORE

I have always grown from my problems and challenges, from the things that don't work out—that's when I've really learned.
CAROL BURNETT

I think these difficult times have helped me to understand better than before how infinitely rich and beautiful life is in every way and that so many things that one goes around worrying about are of no importance whatsoever.

ISAK DINESEN

When you get into a tight place and everything goes against you, till it seems as though you could not hang on a minute longer, never give up then, for that is just the place and time that the tide will turn.

HARRIET BEECHER STOWE

Expect trouble as an inevitable part of life and repeat to yourself the most comforting words of all: This, too, shall pass.

ANN LANDERS

If you want a place in the sun, you've got to put up with a few blisters.

ABIGAIL VAN BUREN

Style

A child develops individuality long before he develops taste. I have seen my kid straggle into the kitchen in the morning with outfits that need only one accessory: an empty gin bottle.

ERMA BOMBECK

I adore wearing gems, but not because they are mine. You can't possess radiance, you can only admire it.

ELIZABETH TAYLOR

Designer clothes worn by children are like snowsuits worn by adults. Few can carry it off successfully.

FRAN LEBOWITZ

One of the goals of life is to try and be in touch with one's most personal themes—the values, ideas, styles, colors that are the touchstones of one's own individual life, its real texture and substance.

GLORIA VANDERBILT

Fashions are born and they die too quickly for anyone to learn to love them.

BETTINA BALLARD

You'd be surprised how much it costs to look this cheap.

DOLLY PARTON

Good taste is the worst vice ever invented.

DAME EDITH SITWELL

Fashion is made to become unfashionable.

COCO CHANEL

Success

The ultimate of being successful is the luxury of giving yourself the time to do what you want to do.

LEONTYNE PRICE

Success is a public affair. Failure is a private funeral.

ROSALIND RUSSELL

Success didn't spoil me; I've always been insufferable.

FRAN LEBOWITZ

Success for me is having ten honeydew melons and eating only the top half of each one.

BARBRA STREISAND

Success is important only to the extent that it puts one in a position to do more things one likes to do.

SARA CALDWELL

The worst part of success is to try to find someone who is happy for you.

BETTE MIDLER

What is success? I think it is a mixture of having a flair for the thing that you are doing; knowing that it is not enough, that you have got to have hard work and a certain sense of purpose.

MARGARET THATCHER

I've always believed that one woman's success can only help another woman's success.

GLORIA VANDERBILT

Success is often achieved by those who don't know that failure is inevitable.

COCO CHANEL

I've never sought success in order to get fame and money; it's the talent and the passion that count in success.

INGRID BERGMAN

To me success means effectiveness in the world, that I am able to carry my ideas and values into the world—that I am able to change it in positive ways.

MAXINE HONG KINGSTON

Success can make you go one of two ways. It can make you a prima donna, or it can smooth the edges, take away the insecurities and let the nice things come out.

BARBARA WALTERS

Success isn't everything but it makes a man stand straight.

LILLIAN HELLMAN

To feel valued, to know, even if only once in a while, that you can do a job well is an absolutely marvelous feeling.

BARBARA WALTERS

Television

Thanks to television, for the first time the young are seeing history made before it is censored by their elders.

MARGARET MEAD

Educational television should be absolutely forbidden. It can only lead to unreasonable expectations and eventual disappointment when your child discovers that the letters of the alphabet do not leap up out of books and dance around the room with royal-blue chickens.

FRAN LEBOWITZ

I'm always amazed that people will actually choose to sit in front of the television and just be savaged by stuff that belittles their intelligence.

ALICE WALKER

Television has proved that people will look at anything rather than each other.

ANN LANDERS

There's a good deal in common between the mind's eye and the t.v. screen, and though the t.v. set has all too often been the boob tube, it could be, it can be, the box of dreams.

URSULA K. LE GUIN

Television could perform a great service in mass education, but there's no indication its sponsors have anything like this on their minds.

TALLULAH BANKHEAD

Even if every program were educational and every advertisement bore the seal of approval of the American Dental Association, we would still have a critical problem. It's not just the programs but the act of watching television hour after hour after hour that's destructive.

ELLEN GOODMAN

Television is actually closer to reality than anything in books. The madness of t.v. is the madness of human life.

CAMILLE PAGLIA

There is no reason to confuse television news with journalism.

NORA EPHRON

T.v. is a language all its own, a land of one-dimensional stereotypes that destroys culture, not adds to it. T.v. is anti-art, a reflection of consumerism that serves the power structure. T.v. is about demographics.

ROSEANNE

Theater

Fundamentally I feel that there is as much difference between the stage and the films as between a piano and a violin. Normally you can't become a virtuoso in both.

ETHEL BARRYMORE

It's one of the tragic ironies of the theater that only one man in it can count on steady work—the night watchman.

TALLULAH BANKHEAD

Every now and then, when you're on stage, you hear the best sound a player can hear. It's the sound you can't get in movies or in television. It is the sound of a wonderful, deep silence that means you've hit them where they live.

SHELLEY WINTERS

Theater is a verb before it is a noun, an act before it is a place.

MARTHA GRAHAM

The theater is the only branch of art much cared for by people of wealth; like canasta, it does away with the bother of talk after dinner.

MARY MCCARTHY

I can't do the same thing every night, the same gestures . . . it's like putting on dirty panties every day.

BRIGITTE BARDOT

The stage was our school, our home, our life.

LILLIAN GISH

Failure in the theater is more dramatic and uglier than any other form of writing. It costs so much, you feel so guilty.

LILLIAN HELLMAN

This play holds the season's record [for early closing], thus far, with a run of four evening performances and one matinee. By an odd coincidence it ran just five performances too many.

DOROTHY PARKER

Tragedy

Sorrow is so easy to express and yet so hard to tell.

JONI MITCHELL

Comedy is tragedy plus time.

CAROL BURNETT

I saw that nothing was permanent. You don't want to possess anything that is dear to you because you might lose it.

YOKO ONO

It's odd that you can get so anesthetized by your own pain or your own problem that you don't quite fully share the hell of someone close to you.

LADY BIRD JOHNSON

I tell myself that God gave my children many gifts—spirit, beauty, intelligence, the capacity to make friends and to inspire respect. There was only one gift he held back—length of life.

ROSE KENNEDY

Misfortune, and recited misfortune in especial, may be prolonged to that point where it ceases to excite pity and arouse only irritation.

DOROTHY PARKER

Travel

Being away from home gave me the chance to look at myself with a jaundiced eye. I learned not to be ashamed of a real hunger for knowledge, something I had always tried to hide, and I came home glad to start in here again with a love for Europe that I am afraid will never leave me.

JACQUELINE KENNEDY ONASSIS

The yearning of the provincial for the capital is a quite exceptional passion. It sets in early, and until it is satisfied it does not let go. It draws its subjects into a strange world where trains and hotels take on an exceptional significance. Many suffering from it become travelers, but perhaps they are aware that travel is simply an extension of that first uprooting, a desire to repeat that first incomparable shock.

MARGARET DRABBLE

Travel seems not just a way of having a good time, but something that every self-respecting citizen ought to undertake, like a high-fiber diet, say, or a deodorant.

JAN MORRIS

We travel, some of us forever, to seek other states, other lives, other souls.

ANAÏS NIN

When traveling with someone, take large doses of patience and tolerance with your morning coffee.

HELEN HAYES

Through travel I first became aware of the outside world; it was through travel that I found my own introspective way into becoming a part of it.

EUDORA WELTY

Before one actually visits them, everyone tends to think of their favorite countries as one grand Disneyland filled with national monuments and historical treasures conveniently laid out for easy viewing, when what they really are filled with, of course, is people going to work, laundromats, and places to buy rat poison.

BETTE MIDLER

Traveling is so complicated. There are so many people everywhere. I make my best journeys on my couch.

COCO CHANEL

Nothing is so awesomely unfamiliar as the familiar that discloses itself at the end of a journey. Nothing shakes the heart so much as meeting—far, far away—what you last met at home.

CYNTHIA OZICK

The more I traveled the more I realized that fear makes strangers of people who should be friends.

SHIRLEY MACLAINE

Truth

You never find yourself until you face the truth.

PEARL BAILEY

The naked truth is always better than the best-dressed lie.

ANN LANDERS

The truth isn't always beauty, but the hunger for it is.

NADINE GORDIMER

Truth is balance, but the opposite of truth, which is unbalance, may not be a lie.

SUSAN SONTAG

Much sheer effort goes into avoiding truth: left to itself, it sweeps in like the tide.

FAY WELDON

The times are so peculiar now, so medieval, so unreasonable, that for the first time in a hundred years truth is really stranger than fiction. Any truth.

GERTRUDE STEIN

No blame should attach to telling the truth. But it does, it does.

ANITA BROOKNER

Truth does not change according to our ability to stomach it emotionally.

FLANNERY O'CONNOR

I am the only real truth I know.

JEAN RHYS

There are no new truths, but only truths that have not been recognized by those who have perceived them without noticing. A truth is something that everyone can be shown to know and to have known, as people say, all along.

MARY MCCARTHY

The best mind-altering drug is truth.

LILY TOMLIN

United States of America

With all our shortcomings, the truth about America carries its own force. When young people—or, indeed, people of all ages—come to this country and look at it for themselves, they see how democracy functions in daily life; see men and women going about their lives without fear, in fields they have chosen.

ELEANOR ROOSEVELT

The big cities of America are becoming Third World countries.

NORA EPHRON

Those of us who shout the loudest about Americanism in making character assassinations are all too frequently those who, by our own words and acts, ignore some of the basic principles of Americanism—

The right to criticize.
The right to hold unpopular beliefs.
The right to protest.
The right of independent thought.

MARGARET CHASE SMITH

It could be so beautiful here if the Americans themselves had not made it so ugly with their big buildings, their millions of cars, and noise.

GRETA GARBO

Give me your tired, your poor,
  Your huddled masses yearning to breathe free,
The wretched refuse of your teeming shore,
Send these, the homeless, tempest-tossed
    to me,
I lift my lamp beside the golden door!

EMMA LAZARUS

I am not belittling the brave pioneer men, but the sunbonnet as well as the sombrero has helped to settle this glorious land of ours.

EDNA FERBER

What the people want is very simple. They want an America as good as its promise.

BARBARA JORDAN

The American Dream is really money.

JILL ROBINSON

America, which has the most glorious present still existing in the world today, hardly stops to enjoy it, in her insatiable appetite for the future.

ANNE MORROW LINDBERGH

Southerners can never resist a losing cause.

MARGARET MITCHELL

Coming to America has always been hard. Thriving in America is harder than ever. But so many things remain the same. And one of them is that the people who, generation to generation, believe America is a finished product are habitually revealed as people whose ideas would have impoverished this country beyond measure. It is foolish to forget where you come from, and that, in the case of the United States, is almost always somewhere else. The true authentic American is a pilgrim with a small 'p' armed with little more than the phrase "I wish . . ."

ANNA QUINDLEN

America is gangsterism for the private profit of the few.

VANESSA REDGRAVE

The American landscape has no foreground and the American mind has no background.

EDITH WHARTON

In America you watch t.v. and think that's totally unreal, then you step outside and it's just the same.

JOAN ARMATRADING

Americans are uneasy with their possessions, guilty about power, all of which is difficult for me to perceive because they are themselves so truly materialistic, so versed in the use of power.

JOAN DIDION

Violence and War

I would rather fight with my hands than my tongue.

DOLLEY MADISON

I'm glad we've been bombed. It makes me feel I can look the East End in the face.

QUEEN ELIZABETH, THE QUEEN MOTHER

The quietly pacifist peaceful always die to make room for men who shout.

ALICE WALKER

Children do not take war seriously as war. War is soldiers and soldiers have not to be war but they have to be soldiers. Which is a nice thing.

GERTRUDE STEIN

Once in a Cabinet we had to deal with the fact that there had been an outbreak of assaults on women at night. One minister suggested a curfew: women should stay home after dark. I said, "But it's the men who are attacking the women. If there's to be a curfew, let the men stay home, not the women."

GOLDA MEIR

It is wise statesmanship which suggests that in time of peace we must prepare for war, and it is no less a wise benevolence that makes preparation in the hour of peace for assuaging the ills that are sure to accompany war.

CLARA BARTON

One is left with the horrible feeling now that war settles *nothing*; that to *win* a war is as disastrous as to lose one.

AGATHA CHRISTIE

You can no more win a war than you can win an earthquake.

JEANNETTE RANKIN

If a woman gets nervous, she'll eat or go shopping. A man will attack a country—it's a whole other way of thinking.

ELAYNE BOOSLER

If it's natural to kill why do men have to go into training to learn how?

JOAN BAEZ

Cogito ergo boom.

SUSAN SONTAG

When men talk about defense, they always claim to be protecting women and children, but they never ask the women and children what they think.

PATRICIA SCHROEDER

The only thing that's been a worse flop than the organization of non-violence has been the organization of violence.

JOAN BAEZ

As a woman I can't go to war, and I refuse to send anyone else.

JEANNETTE RANKIN

Wealth/Poverty

No one would remember the Good Samaritan if he'd only had good intentions. He had money as well.

MARGARET THATCHER

The rich have a passion for bargains as lively as it is pointless.

FRANÇOISE SAGAN

There are people who have money and people who are rich.

COCO CHANEL

Hollywood money isn't money. It's congealed snow, melts in your hand, and there you are.

DOROTHY PARKER

It's easy to be independent when you've got money. But to be independent when you haven't got a thing—that's the Lord's test.

MAHALIA JACKSON

Children do not really need money. After all, they don't have to pay rent or send mailgrams.

FRAN LEBOWITZ

One should, I think, always give children money, for they will spend it for themselves far more profitably than we can ever spend it for them.

ROSE MACAULAY

A fool and his money are soon married.

CAROLYN WELLS

Money is always there, but the pockets change.

GERTRUDE STEIN

Hunger makes a thief of any man.

PEARL S. BUCK

I was so poor I didn't know where my next husband was coming from.

MAE WEST

Where large sums of money are concerned, it is advisable to trust nobody.

AGATHA CHRISTIE

I came from a poor and humble background. I did not come from a family of people who had a poverty view of the world. I came from people who viewed the world as attainable.

FAYE WATTLETON

I think women are just as moved by appearance [as men are], but they are willing to accept a situation where the man is less attractive because of the "who earns the bread" situation.

MADONNA

Hungry people cannot be good at learning or producing anything, except perhaps violence.

PEARL BAILEY

The man has the burden of the money. It's needed day after day. More and more of it. For ordinary things and for life. That's why holidays are a hard time for him. Another hard time is the weekend, when he's not making money or furthering himself.

GRACE PALEY

The power of money is a distinctly male power. Money speaks, but it speaks with a male voice.

ANDREA DWORKIN

Money has nothing to do with style at all, but naturally it helps every situation.

DIANA VREELAND

Money is the root of all good.

AYN RAND

Witticisms

It's a man's world, and you men can have it.

KATHERINE ANNE PORTER

I don't deserve any credit for turning the other cheek as my tongue is always in it.

FLANNERY O'CONNOR

A fox is a wolf who sends flowers.

RUTH WESTON

When a man gives his opinion he's a man. When a woman gives her opinion she's a bitch.

BETTE DAVIS

A woman needs a man like a fish needs a net.

CYNTHIA HEIMEL

Boys don't make passes at female smartasses.

LETTY COTTIN POGREBIN

A Woman's Nature

Women want men, careers, money, children, friends, luxury, comfort, independence, freedom, respect, love, and a three-dollar pantyhose that won't run.

PHYLLIS DILLER

A man never knows how to say goodbye; a woman never knows when to say it.

HELEN ROWLAND

I'm not happy, I'm cheerful. There's a difference. A happy woman has no cares at all. A cheerful woman has cares but has learned how to deal with them.

BEVERLY SILLS

A man has to be Joe McCarthy to be called ruthless. All a woman has to do is put you on hold.

MARLO THOMAS

Girls got balls. They're just a little higher up, that's all.

JOAN JETT

The especial genius of women I believe to be electrical in movement, intuitive in function, and spiritual in tendency.

MARGARET FULLER

Character contributes to beauty. It fortifies a woman as her youth fades. A mode of conduct, a standard of courage, discipline, fortitude, and integrity can do a great deal to make a woman beautiful.

JACQUELINE BISSET

All women hustle. Women watch faces, voices, gestures, moods. . . . She's the person who has to survive through cunning.

MARGE PIERCY

Women on Men

The trouble about man is twofold. He cannot learn truths which are too complicated; he forgets truths which are too simple.

REBECCA WEST

I'd never seen men hold each other. I thought the only thing they were allowed to do was shake hands or fight.

RITA MAE BROWN

If you never want to see a man again, say, "I love you. I want to marry you. I want to have children"—they leave skid marks.

RITA RUDNER

American men say "I love you" as part of the conversation.

LIV ULLMAN

I get bored with a man who isn't emotionally conversant with himself.

SHIRLEY MACLAINE

Imagine how often women who think they are displaying a positive quality—connecting—are misjudged by men who perceive them as revealing a lack of independence, which the men regard as synonymous with incompetence and insecurity.

DEBORAH TANNEN

All men seek esteem; the best by lifting themselves, which is hard to do; the rest by shoving others down, which is much easier.

MARY RENAULT

Some men break your heart in two,
Some men fawn and flatter,
Some men never look at you,
And that cleans up the matter.

DOROTHY PARKER

Any woman can fool a man if she wants to and if he's in love with her.

AGATHA CHRISTIE

All men are not slimy warthogs. Some men are silly giraffes, some woebegone puppies, some insecure frogs. But if one is not careful, those slimy warthogs can ruin it for others.

CYNTHIA HEIMEL

I don't hate men, I just wish they'd try harder. They all want to be heroes and all we want is for them to stay at home and help with the housework and the kids. That's not the kind of heroism they enjoy.

JEANETTE WINTERSON

Man reaches the highest point of lovableness at twelve to seventeen—to get it back, in a second flowering, at the age of seventy to ninety.

ISAK DINESEN

Men say they love independence in a woman, but they don't waste a second demolishing it brick by brick.

CANDICE BERGEN

A girl can wait for the right man to come along, but in the meantime, that still doesn't mean she can't have a wonderful time with all the wrong ones.

CHER

I have always wanted to be a man, if only for the reason that I would like to have gauged the value of my intellect.

MARGOT ASQUITH

When a man wants to deceive you, he'll find a way of escape through the tiniest holes.

COLETTE

It's not the men in my life that count; it's the life in my men.

MAE WEST

Men don't like independent women.

SHIRLEY CHISHOLM

My idea of a screamingly boring man is a chap who doesn't like the company of women.

ANNE EDWARDS

He was every other inch a gentleman.

REBECCA WEST

Most women set out to try to change a man, and when they have changed him they do not like him.

MARLENE DIETRICH

A man speaks only when driven to speech by something outside himself—like, for instance, he can't find any clean socks.

JEAN KERR

Whether women are better than men I cannot say—but I can say they are certainly no worse.

GOLDA MEIR

Beware of men who cry. It's true that men who cry are sensitive to and in touch with feelings, but the only feelings they tend to be sensitive to and in touch with are their own.

NORA EPHRON

Though men may be deep, mentally they are slow.

CAMILLE PAGLIA

The only time a woman really succeeds in changing a man is when he is a baby.

NATALIE WOOD

Men know everything—all of them—all the time—no matter how stupid or inexperienced or arrogant or ignorant they are.

ANDREA DWORKIN

Inside every adult male is a denied little boy.

NANCY FRIDAY

Beware of a man with manners.

EUDORA WELTY

When you love a man, he becomes more than a body. His physical limbs expand, and his outline recedes, vanishes. He is rich and sweet and right. He is part of the world, the atmosphere, the blue sky and the blue water.

GWENDOLYN BROOKS

Getting along with men isn't what's truly important. The vital knowledge is how to get along with a man, one man.

PHYLLIS MCGINLEY

Women on Women

One is not born a woman, one becomes one.

SIMONE DE BEAUVOIR

I think being a woman is like being Irish. . . . Everyone says you're important and nice but you take second place all the time.

IRIS MURDOCH

Women are the only oppressed group in our society that lives in intimate association with their oppressors.

EVELYN CUNNINGHAM

A woman can do anything. She can be traditionally feminine and that's all right; she can work, she can stay at home; she can be aggressive; she can be passive; she can be any way she wants with a man. But whenever there are the kinds of choices there are today, unless you have some solid base, life can be frightening.

BARBARA WALTERS

But if God had wanted us to think just with our wombs, why did He give us a brain?

CLARE BOOTHE LUCE

I have some women friends but I prefer men. Don't trust women. There is a built-in competition between women.

EDNA O'BRIEN

We have no faith in ourselves. I have never met a woman who, deep down in her core, really believes she has great legs. And if she suspects that she *might* have great legs, then she's convinced that she has a shrill voice and no neck.

CYNTHIA HEIMEL

How wrong it is for woman to expect the man to build the world she wants, rather than set out to create it herself.

ANAÏS NIN

Women have served all these centuries as looking glasses possessing the . . . power of reflecting the figure of man at twice its natural size.

VIRGINIA WOOLF

A woman has to be twice as good as a man to go half as far.

FANNIE HURST

One of the sad commentaries on the way women are viewed in our society is that we have to fit one category. I have never felt that I had to be in one category.

FAYE WATTLETON

I hear the singing of the lives of women. The clear mystery, the offering, and pride.

MURIEL RUKEYSER

Women are the only exploited group in history who have been idealized into powerlessness.

ERICA JONG

Women, if the soul of the nation is to be saved, I believe that you must become its soul.

CORETTA SCOTT KING

Women on Themselves

I'm tough, ambitious, and I know exactly what I want. If that makes me a bitch, okay.

MADONNA

I will not be just a tourist in the world of images, just watching images passing by which I cannot live in, make love to, possess as permanent sources of joy and ecstasy.

ANAÏS NIN

I have bursts of being a lady, but it doesn't last long.

SHELLEY WINTERS

I never intended to become a run-of-the-mill person.

BARBARA JORDAN

I am what I am. Take it or leave me alone.

ROSARIO MORALES

Work

The days you work are the best days.

GEORGIA O'KEEFFE

The word *career* is a divisive word. It's a word that divides the normal life from business or professional life.

GRACE PALEY

Always be smarter than the people who hire you.

LENA HORNE

Find something you're passionate about and keep tremendously interested in it.

JULIA CHILD

The test for whether or not you can hold a job should not be the arrangement of your chromosomes.

BELLA ABZUG

One and one is two, and two and two is four, and five will get you ten if you know how to work it.

MAE WEST

When men reach their sixties and retire, they go to pieces. Women go right on cooking.

GAIL SHEEHY

No office anywhere on earth is so puritanical, impeccable, elegant, sterile, or incorruptible as not to contain the yeast for at least one affair, probably more. You can say it couldn't happen *here*, but just let a yeast riser into the place and the first thing you know—bread!

HELEN GURLEY BROWN

Nobody ever drowned in his own sweat.
                                ANN LANDERS

If a woman is sent to the Middle East . . . will she be able to
cover stories there as well as a man? Yes. They may think
she's a whore, but often they will talk to her more openly
than to a male reporter.
                                LINDA ELLERBEE

Laziness may appear attractive, but work gives satisfaction.
                                ANNE FRANK

I could have succeeded much easier in my career had I been
a man.
                                HENRIETTA GREEN

I've got a woman's ability to stick to a job and get on with it
when everyone else walks off and leaves it.
                                MARGARET THATCHER

Neither woman nor man lives by work, or love, alone. . . . The
human self defines itself and grows through love *and* work: All
psychology before and after Freud boils down to that.
                                BETTY FRIEDAN

This became a credo of mine: Attempt the impossible in order
to improve your work.
                                BETTE DAVIS

I look back on my life like a good day's work, it was done and I am satisfied with it.

GRANDMA MOSES

I have yet to hear a man ask for advice on how to combine marriage and a career.

GLORIA STEINEM

Where I was born, and where and how I lived is unimportant. It is what I have done and where I have been that should be of interest.

GEORGIA O'KEEFFE

I believe in my work and the joy of it. You have to be with the work and the work has to be with you. It absorbs you totally and you absorb it totally. Everything must fall by the wayside by comparison.

LOUISE NEVELSON

I don't know anything about luck. I've never banked on it, and I'm afraid of people who do. Luck to me is something else: hard work—and realizing what is opportunity and what isn't.

LUCILLE BALL

A job is not a career. I think I started out with a job. It turned into a career and changed my life. A career means long hours, travel, frustration and plain hard work and finally perhaps a realization that you can't have it all.

BARBARA WALTERS

I don't know that there are any short cuts to doing a good job.

SANDRA DAY O'CONNOR

The secret of joy in work is contained in one word—excellence. To know how to do something well is to enjoy it.

PEARL S. BUCK

The World

The beauty of the world, which is so soon to perish, has two edges, one of laughter, one of anguish, cutting the heart asunder.

VIRGINIA WOOLF

Perhaps when distant people on other planets pick up some wave-length of ours all they hear is a continuous scream.

IRIS MURDOCH

If the world were a logical place, men would ride side-saddle.

RITA MAE BROWN

When you make a world tolerable for yourself, you make a world tolerable for others.

ANAÏS NIN

The more the wonders of the world become inaccessible, the more intensely do its curiosities affect us.

COLETTE

Writers

Life can't defeat a writer who is in love with writing, for life itself is a writer's lover until death.

EDNA FERBER

I wanted to use what I was, to be what I was born to be— not to have a "career," but to be that straightforward obvious unmistakable animal, a writer.

CYNTHIA OZICK

My characters never die screaming in rage. They attempt to pull themselves back together and go on. And that's basically a conservative view of life.

JANE SMILEY

The writer should never be ashamed of staring. There is nothing that does not require his attention.

FLANNERY O'CONNOR

The narratives . . . that keep me company, along with the living, breathing people in my life, were those that talked honestly about growing up black in America. They burst into my silence, and in my head, they shouted and chattered and whispered and sang together. I am writing . . . to become part of that unruly conversation, and to bring my experience back to the community of minds that made it possible.

LORENE CARY

They're fancy talkers about themselves, writers. If I had to give young writers advice, I would say don't listen to writers talk about writing or themselves.

LILLIAN HELLMAN

The novelist, afraid his ideas may be foolish, slyly puts them in the mouth of some other fool and reserves the right to disavow him.

DIANE JOHNSON

I once said in an interview that every word she [Lillian Hellman] writes is a lie, including "and" and "the."

MARY MCCARTHY

I'm not happy when I'm writing, but I'm more unhappy when I'm not.

FANNIE HURST

There is one last thing to remember: *writers are always selling somebody out.*

JOAN DIDION

A writer does not always write in the ways others wish. . . . I am giving myself permission to write books that do not depend on anyone's liking them, because what I want to do is write better.

TONI MORRISON

Why don't you write books people can read?

NORA JOYCE TO HER HUSBAND, JAMES

I continue to create because writing is a labor of love and also an act of defiance, a way to light a candle in a gale wind.

ALICE CHILDRESS

Writers should be read, but neither seen nor heard.

DAPHNE DU MAURIER

It is not my experience that society hates and fears the writer, or that society adulates the writer. Instead my experience is the common one, that society places the writer so far beyond the pale that society does not regard the writer at all.

ANNIE DILLARD

I began to ration my writing, for fear I would dream through life as my father had done. I was afraid I had inherited a poisoned gene from him, a vocation without a gift.

MAVIS GALLANT

It's not the college degree that makes a writer. The great thing is to have a story to tell.

POLLY ADLER

Whenever I'm asked why Southern writers particularly have a penchant for writing about freaks, I say it is because we are still able to recognize one. To be able to recognize a freak, you have to have some conception of the whole man, and in the South the general conception of man is still, in the main, theological.

FLANNERY O'CONNOR

Quite often you want to tell somebody your dream, your nightmare. Well, nobody wants to hear about someone else's dream, good or bad; nobody wants to walk around with it. The writer is always tricking the reader into listening to the dream.

JOAN DIDION

I don't know everything, I just do everything.

TONI MORRISON

Each story is like a new challenge or a new adventure and I don't find help anywhere, or look for it anywhere, except inside.

EUDORA WELTY

Literary men, when they like women at all, do not want literary women. What they want is girls.

MURIEL SPARK

Deliver me from writers who say the way they live doesn't matter. I'm not sure a bad person can write a good book. If art doesn't make us better, then what on earth is it for?

ALICE WALKER

I have spent so long erecting partitions around the part of me that writes—learning how to close the door on it when ordinary life intervenes, how to close the door on ordinary life when it's time to start writing again—that I'm not sure I could fit the two parts of me back together now.

ANNE TYLER

Writing

Nothing you write, if you hope to be any good, will ever come out as you first hoped.

LILLIAN HELLMAN

Writing is the great vocation of the dispossessed.

MARY GORDON

Your life story would not make a good book. Don't even try.

FRAN LEBOWITZ

Writing novels preserves you in a state of innocence—a lot passes you by—simply because your attention is otherwise diverted.

ANITA BROOKNER

A work in progress quickly becomes feral. It reverts to a wild state overnight. It is barely domesticated, a mustang on which you one day fastened a halter, but which now you cannot catch. It is a lion you cage in your study. As the work grows, it gets harder to control; it is a lion growing in strength. You must visit it every day and reassert your mastery over it. If you skip a day, you are, quite rightly, afraid to open the door to its room.

ANNIE DILLARD

I have always hated biography, and more especially, autobiography. If biography, the writer invariable finds it necessary to plaster the subject with praises, flattery, and adulation and to invest him with all the Christian graces. If autobiography, the same plan is followed, but the writer apologizes for it.

CAROLYN WELLS

If technique is of no interest to a writer, I doubt that the writer is an artist.

MARIANNE MOORE

I find that most people know what a story is until they sit down to write one.

FLANNERY O'CONNOR

Another unsettling element in modern art is that common symptom of immaturity, the dread of doing what has been done before.

EDITH WHARTON

A woman must have money and a room of her own if she is to write fiction.

VIRGINIA WOOLF

It's easy to lose the energy you need for a long piece unless the characters are surprising you and showing you something new every week or even every month or every other paragraph.

ALICE MCDERMOTT

The best time for planning a book is while you're doing the dishes.

AGATHA CHRISTIE

I like to think of what happens to characters in good novels and stories as knots—things keep knotting up. And by the end of the story, readers see an "unknotting" of sorts. Not what they expect, not the easy answers you get on t.v., not wash-and-wear philosophies, but a reproduction of believable emotional experiences.

TERRY MCMILLAN

Keep a diary and one day it'll keep you.

MAE WEST

Writing a novel is not merely going on a shopping expedition across the border to an unreal land: it is hours and years spent in the factories, the streets, the cathedrals of the imagination.

JANET FRAME

I think long and hard about what my novels should do. They should clarify the roles that have become obscured, they ought to identify those things in the past that are useful and those that are not and they ought to give nourishment.

TONI MORRISON

Men's novels are about how to get power. Killing and so on, or winning and so on.

MARGARET ATWOOD

Men are so accustomed to being flattered in books by women that simple honesty comes as a shock and they register [it] as biased and unfair.

FAY WELDON

A man would never get the notion of writing a book on the peculiar situation of the human male.

SIMONE DE BEAUVOIR

Bibliography

Adler, Bill. *The Quotable Conservative*. New York: Birch Lane Press, 1996.

Adler, Gloria. *She Said, She Said*. New York: Avon Books, 1995.

Anderson, Peggy. *Great Quotes from Great Women*. Franklin Lakes, NJ: Career Press, 1997.

Andrews, Robert. *Cassell Dictionary of Contemporary Quotations*. London, England: Cassell, 1996.

Augarde, Tony. *The Oxford Dictionary of Modern Quotations*. Oxford, England: Oxford University Press, 1991.

Ayres, Alex. *The Wit and Wisdom of Eleanor Roosevelt: An A-Z Compendium of Quotations*. New York: Meridian, 1996.

Beilenson, Evelyn L. and Tenenbaum, Ann. *Wit and Wisdom of Famous American Women*. New York: Peter Pauper Press, Inc., 1995.

Biggs, Mary. *Women's Words: The Columbia Book of Quotations by Women*. New York: Columbia University Press, 1996.

Byrne, Robert. *The 637 Best Things Anybody Ever Said*. New York: Fawcett Crest, 1982.

————. *1,911 Best Things Anybody Ever Said*. New York: Fawcett Columbine, 1988.

Conny, Beth Mende. *Winning Women: Quotations on Sports, Health & Fitness*. New York: Peter Pauper Press, Inc. 1993.

Edmonson, Catherine M. *365 Women's Reflections on Men*. Holbrook, MA: Adams Media Corporation, 1997.

Eisen, Armand. *America: Of Thee I Sing*. Kansas City, MO: Andrews and McMeel, 1995.

———. *Witty Women: Wise, Wicked, & Wonderful Words*. Kansas City, MO: Andrews and McMeel, 1994.

Exley, Helen. *The Best of Father Quotations*. New York: Exley Giftbooks, 1995.

———. *The Best of Women's Quotations*. New York: Exley Giftbooks, 1993.

Feuer, Susan. *Believing in Ourselves: The Wisdom of Women*. Kansas City, MO: Ariel Books/Andrews and McMeel, 1997.

Ginsberg, Susan. *Family Wisdom: The 2,000 Most Important Things Ever Said About Parenting, Children, and Family Life*. New York: Columbia University Press, 1996.

Hale, Helen. *The Art & Artist's Quotation Book: A Literary Companion*. Great Britain: Robert Hale Limited, 1995.

Johnson, Diane J. *Proud Sisters: The Wisdom & Wit of African-American Women*. White Plains, NY: Peter Pauper Press, Inc., 1995.

Johnson, Venice. *Voices of the Dream: African-American Women Speak*. San Francisco: Chronicle Books, 1995.

Kipfer, Barbara Ann. *Bartlett's Book of Business Quotations*. New York: Little, Brown and Company, 1994.

———. *Bartlett's Book of Love Quotations*. New York: Little, Brown and Company, 1994.

Maggio, Rosalie. *The Beacon Book of Quotations by Women*. Boston: Beacon Press, 1992.

———. *The New Beacon Book of Quotations by Women*. Boston: Beacon Press, 1996.

Malloy, Merrit. *Irish-American Funny Quotes*. New York: Sterling Publishing Company, Inc., 1994.

Metcalf, Fred. *The Penguin Dictionary of Modern Humorous Quotations*. New York: Penguin Books, 1986.

The Princeton Institute. *21st Century Dictionary of Quotations*. New York: Dell Publishing, 1993.

The Quotable Woman: Witty, Poignant, and Insightful Observations from Notable Women. Philadelphia: Running Press, 1991.

Reagan, Michael, and Phillips, Bob. *The All-American Quote Book*. Eugene, OR: Harvest House Publishers, 1995.

Reed, Maxine. *And Baby Makes Three: Wise and Witty Observations on the Joy of Parenthood*. Chicago: Contemporary Books, 1995.

Schwartz, Ronald B. *The 501 Best and Worst Things Ever Said About Marriage*. New York: Carol Publishing Group, 1995.

Sheehan, Sean. *Dictionary of Irish Quotations*. Cork, Ireland: Mercier Press Ltd., 1993.

Simpson, James B. *Simpson's Contemporary Quotations*. Boston: Houghton Mifflin, 1988.

Stein, Melissa. *The Wit and Wisdom of Women*. Philadelphia: Running Press, 1993.

Stibbs, Anne. *A Woman's Place: Quotations About Women*. New York: Avon Books, 1992.

Wylie, Betty Jane. *Men! Quotations About Men, by Women*. Toronto, Ontario: Key Porter Books, 1993.

Index